insight text guide

Sue Sciortino

Montana 1948

Larry Watson

First published in 1999. Reprinted in 2003, 2004, 2008, 2012, 2015, 2017, 2018, 2019, 2020, 2021.

Insight Publications Pty Ltd
3/350 Charman Road
Cheltenham VIC 3192
Australia
Tel: +61 3 8571 4950
Fax: +61 3 8571 0257
Email: books@insightpublications.com.au

www.insightpublications.com.au

National Library of Australia Cataloguing-in-Publication entry:
Sciortino, Sue
Insight text guide: Larry Watson's Montana 1948
For secondary and tertiary students.
ISBN 9781875882311
1. Watson, Larry. Montana 1948.
2. Watson, Larry—Criticism and interpretation.
I. Title. (Series: Insight text guide).
813.54

Other ISBNs:
9781922378521 (digital)
9781922378538 (bundle: print + digital)

Cover design: The Modern Art Production Group

Printed in Australia by Ligare

contents

CHARACTER MAP

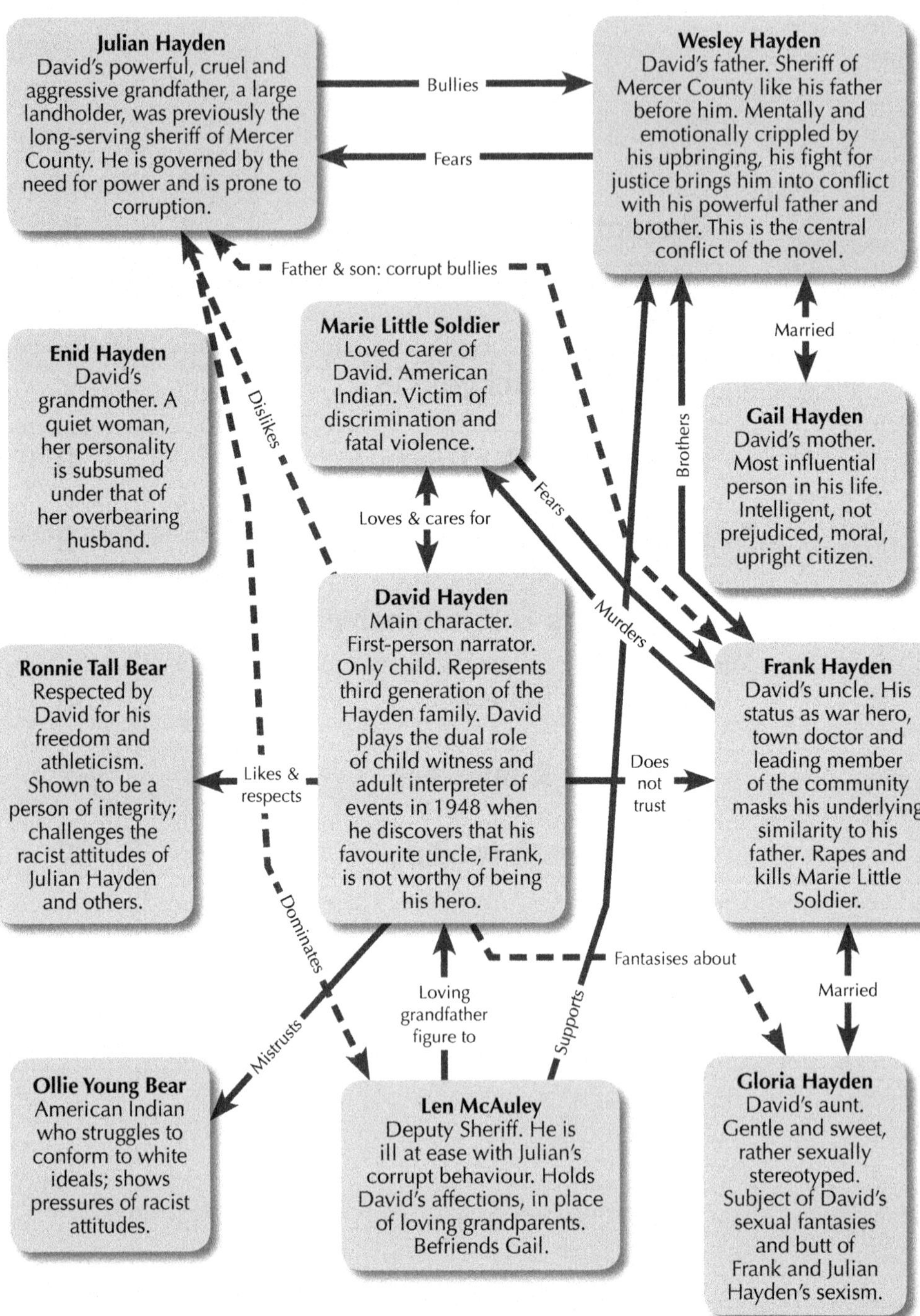

INTRODUCTION

Larry Watson was born in Rugby, North Dakota. Like his grandfather before him, his father was the sheriff of this small town in northeastern North Dakota and Watson has drawn upon this background for *Montana 1948*, a novel which topped the bestseller lists in the United States and won the National Fiction Prize there in 1993. Watson pursued a PhD in creative writing at the University of Utah, then taught at the University of Wisconsin. He is now pursuing a full-time career as a novelist.

The novel is set in a small town in northeastern Montana, a countryside that epitomises the tales and action of Wild West movies. The Indians no longer wear war paint and ride the plains brandishing spears and tomahawks; they are collected together on small reservations, dispossessed of their land and their heritage, defeated by the superior power of the white settlers. It is against a background of racial prejudice that the incidents of the drama are played out. When twelve-year-old David Hayden's uncle is accused of the sexual abuse of Indian women, the family must choose between loyalty and justice.

David's craving to be included in adult matters costs him his childhood innocence in many ways and affects his sexual development at this critical time when he is on the threshold of sexual maturity. His love for Marie Little Soldier, the Indian housekeeper, who is also his carer, is tinged with sexual attraction. When she dies, it seems to David that the freedom and open affection that she has seemed to represent for him has been compromised. He is irreparably damaged by the revelations of that summer.

The author explores the themes of innocence and experience, not just through the child, but also through his father who faces deep conflicts over family loyalties and his responsibilities to uphold the law. This shows him that moral choices are not clear cut, that there are not always clear alternatives and that lines of principle can be blurred.

CONTEXT & BACKGROUND

Montana

Montana is a northern state of the United States of America, close to the border of Canada. It became the forty-first state in 1889. The novel is set in the northeast corner of the state in the flat plains area where the land is barren and windblown. The average daily maximum temperatures range from around 0°C in winter to around 30°C in summer.

Helena is the capital of Montana but Billings (p.18) is Montana's largest city with a population of more than 100,000, almost an eighth of the total population of the state. Only three other states – Alaska, Texas and California – have an area larger than Montana and only two states – Alaska and Wyoming – have a lower population density. Cattle and sheep outnumber people in Montana by a ratio of 100 to one.

Montana and white explorers

The first white explorers to the area were members of the Lewis and Clark Expedition in 1804–6, which was the first overland expedition to the Pacific coast and back. Montana was not really opened up until the 1860s with the discovery of gold. Cattle and sheep grazing began in the area shortly after, the herds driven overland from Texas, leading to protracted and bitter battles with the Indians who opposed incursions on their hunting grounds and decimation of the buffalo. Farmers followed in the 1900s but after a few good harvests the land's harshness meant a failure of crops and many farmers left the area.

Native Americans – Indians

The Native Americans were misnamed Indians by Christopher Columbus who thought he had discovered a new route to India. For some time they were called Red Indians or Redskins, because of their copper-coloured skin, but this is now recognised as derogatory and racist, especially as skin colour has been the basis of discrimination against the Native Americans as inferior to whites. The novel reflects the attitudes of the day with Julian referring crudely to Indian women as 'red meat'. The term 'Indian' is retained here as it is used throughout the novel.

Sioux resistance

Before Europeans arrived, the tribes of the Great Plains area populated the country. They were essentially big game hunters, particularly of the buffalo. The main nations to occupy the Montana area were the Cheyenne and the Dakota, properly known as the Sioux. Marie Little Soldier is a Hunkpapa Sioux of the Lakota or Teton division of the Sioux nation. Of all the Plains tribes, the Sioux were the most resolute in resisting white men's incursions upon their land. They were particularly incensed by the government's attempt to build a road to Bozeman, across their favourite hunting grounds in the Bighorn Mountains. In 1865–67 Chief Red Cloud led thousands of Sioux warriors in a campaign to halt the road's construction. On 21 December 1866, a band under Chief High Backbone was responsible for the Fetterman Massacre, a battle in which more than eighty government soldiers were trapped and killed near Fort Phil Kearny. The United States government eventually agreed to abandon the Bozeman Trail and guaranteed the Sioux exclusive possession of the area in South Dakota, west of the Missouri River.

However, when gold was discovered in the Black Hills of South Dakota, thousands of miners disregarded agreements and swarmed into the Sioux reservation, thus precipitating another round of hostilities. In 1876 George Custer and his men were defeated and slain at the Battle of Little Bighorn and the Nez Perce nation won a battle in the Big Hole Basin in 1877. (See References & Reading for a website giving details of Custer's Last Stand.)

Sioux defeat and reservations

Despite their victories, the Indians were overwhelmed and ceased fighting in 1877, most returning to their reservations with the exception of two of the great Indian chiefs, Crazy Horse (killed in 1877) and Sitting Bull (killed in 1890). Finally, though, the US troops' massacre of Sioux men, women and children at the Battle of Wounded Knee in December 1890 marked the end of all Sioux resistance to white domination. (See References & Reading for a website giving details of the Battle of Wounded Knee.)

The reservations are tracts of land, usually very poor, unproductive and even hostile, that the US government allocated to the Native Americans. These were administered by the Federal Government and meant that these proud, independent people lost control over their own lives. Today, two-thirds of the Native Americans live on these reservations.

The Indians of Bentrock

Key point

The dispossession of American Indian lands and thus their failure to survive on their own terms was little understood by whites in 1948. The Indians were a marginalised minority not accepted as part of town communities because of their race. Their culture was not seen as a valid alternative to white Westernised ideas and learning.

Throughout *Montana 1948*, the Indians of Bentrock are not the romanticised Hollywood representation of this proud people 'mounted on war ponies, streaked with war paint, bristling with feathers, and brandishing bows and arrows' (p.101). The attitude of the white community in 1948 towards the Indians was still similar to that of the settlers who 'tamed' the land in the previous century. However, there was an additional element: the developing view that Indians were 'useless', not functional members of society in white terms. These are the feelings of Wesley Hayden towards their 'ignorance' while Frank exploits the women sexually and Julian Hayden regards the women as merely 'red meat'.

World War II

Key point

Whilst no part of World War II was fought on the mainland of the United States, the human cost was deeply felt as US forces served between 1941 and 1945 – their estimated losses were 211,987. Most families were affected in some way by the trauma of war.

Frank Hayden served his country and was welcomed home as a war hero while Wesley Hayden, as many men were, was unfit for active duty and was left behind with the women and children. As a consequence he is scarred because his father thought he was less than a man.

The narrator observes that the relief of the war's end was still being felt and when the soldiers came home 'they wanted nothing more than to work their farms and ranches and to live quietly with their families' (p.16). The novel demonstrates that this was an ambitious aim and, also, that anyone who disturbed that peace was likely to be unpopular. When Wesley Hayden stirs up the community over his brother's sexual assault of Indian women, it rejects him.

Although many women went to work during the war to keep the factories and other services going in the absence of the men, after the war they were encouraged, as never before, to leave the workforce and become housewives and mothers. The baby boomers, the largest generation of children ever born in the western world, were the result of this policy. Gail Hayden, however, is a full-time secretary who has only one child. Further, countries like America and Australia were then on the edge of an economic boom based on primary products and consumerism which glamorised the role of mother and encouraged the purchase of numerous new domestic appliances.

GENRE, STYLE & STRUCTURE

Montana 1948 reconstructs the events of one summer in 1948 for the reader. It is a chronological narrative told by an adult narrator, David Hayden, who recounts events from the perspectives of himself as a twelve-year-old boy and an adult. It is a story of a boy on the threshold of adolescence, awakening to maturity and finding that the adult world is complex and not always fair or just.

Larry Watson achieves a balance of fine writing and suspense while recreating David's painful realisation that maturity brings pain and suffering. As narration progresses, the reader gradually realises the extent of David's psychological damage, sustained from being an indirect participant in the fate of his family.

First-person narrator

Key point

The main narrator is the twelve-year-old David Hayden who plays a double role. He eavesdrops on the adults to learn about important events and then pretends ignorance of what is happening.

This strategy of using a first-person narrator, 'I', allows the author to establish a firsthand, reliable account by the protagonist. Indeed, as the action progresses, there is no evidence that David Hayden is unreliable, but he does both filter the story and impress his own views of people and events on the reader.

The adult narrator

Although speaking directly in both the Prologue and Epilogue, and the early part of the novel in which the setting is established and the main characters introduced, the adult narrator only occasionally intrudes, usually at crucial points of the story, to point out how some things might have been different. For example:

> If I had left the porch and followed Frank's steps down the front walk – I would never have heard the conversation between my father and mother, and perhaps I would have lived out my life with an illusion about my family and perhaps even the human community. Certainly I could not tell this story. (pp.44–45)

Note other points where the adult narrator speaks directly to the reader and see also the Chapter-by-Chapter Analysis.

Structure

The novel opens with a Prologue, which foreshadows the action and contributes to the building of suspense before the story begins. It closes with an Epilogue in which the adult narrator summarises the aftermath of the summer of 1948.

The story is divided into three more or less equal parts without chapter divisions. The action is divided into smaller, self-contained parts which mark the progression of events. Each part ends at a crucial point of development in the story:

- Part One ends with David aware that his father, Wesley, knows that Frank, his brother, is guilty of raping defenceless Indian women.
- Part Two ends with the Wesley's realisation that now Frank is guilty of murdering a defenceless Indian woman – Marie Little Soldier.
- Part Three ends with the twelve-year-old David's naive belief that his uncle's suicide has solved all outstanding problems.

Much of the story is revealed only through the narrator's eavesdropping. The author uses these occasions as structuring points to advance the action and the reader must trust that David accurately records what he overhears.

Commentary on structure

1. The Prologue is extremely important in quickly establishing the drama, the authority of the narrator, and Watson's mastery over language.
2. The flashbacks provide a very economical retelling of the events as they are focussed on the most important incidents, on significant character responses and on important changes in attitudes.
3. The use of first-person narration heightens the drama. We often share young David's limited viewpoint and his urgent desire to discover what is going on.
4. The three main sections of the novel mark stages in David's loss of childhood innocence, which is linked with disillusionment and loss of faith in adults. (Childhood innocence tends to cling to hope for simple solutions that will maintain the status quo in the family.)
5. Most of the events are unfolded in chronological order, but not all. For example, David witnesses Uncle Frank's visit to the house at the time of Marie's death, but this is only revealed later. What effects are gained?
6. While the Epilogue reveals the fates of characters after the main events, it is also very important in revealing ways in which the adult David has been affected. This becomes not only a novel about the inevitable loss of childhood innocence but also the tale of an adult irreparably harmed. Just how harmed is left for the reader to discern.
7. There is also an internal structure as the short episodes are carefully arranged. For example, pp.66–82 in Section Two comment on masculine toughness and Uncle Frank's preference for Indian women then show David's own growing sexual awareness – one delicate and the other linked with violence. Consider the effects of juxtaposition of important scenes like these.
8. Many episodes are recounted without direct guidance from the adult narrator as to how to interpret the incident, or a character's behaviour. This contributes to the complexity and subtlety of the novel and leaves room for different interpretations/readings.

CHAPTER-BY-CHAPTER ANALYSIS

Prologue (pp.11–12)

An image of a movie screen imaginatively projects everything that remains in the narrator's mind, the varying scenes from the Montana summer of 1948 in the small, fictional town of Bentrock, a name which becomes a signifier for the moral standards of its citizens. This is a town close in history to the great Indian battles of the nineteenth century when the white man wished to extend his control over the northern lands and, thus, assume control over the Indian peoples too. In the aftermath, the people of small settlement towns like Bentrock lived with the racial and social consequences of such a history.

The metaphor of the movie screen is strengthened with the similes that follow. The first is the Sioux picture calendar on buffalo hide which records events pictorially all together. The second is the tapestry, a powerful symbol that here conjures up an image of a patchwork wherein all scenes are reproduced simultaneously in the hope that they can be better understood. Now that his parents are dead, the narrator can reproduce the pain of that Montana summer of 1948 in an effort to see the awful events laid out before him in a seamless whole.

Part One (pp.15–54)

Key point

The opening provides a framework for the story, describes the landscape and introduces the central characters.

The first-person narrator opens his story with a detailed description of where the story takes place. Bentrock, Mercer County, is a small town in northern United States of America and the author's choice of the name is obviously meant to be symbolic. It is in 'bent rock' that the scenes of twisted morality and skewed justice are to take place. The landscape is bleak in this flat, plains area where the inhabitants are exposed to the extremes of the elements with freezing winters and short, hot summers. Montana is a large state which shares its northern border with Canada; the north-eastern corner has none of the beauty of the high Rocky Mountains in the west of the state. The ground is bare, unrelieved by natural vegetation. Across this barren land, winds blow relentlessly. This bleak setting provides an appropriate backdrop for the moral dilemmas that the characters face.

The time, post–World War II, is important. Returned soldiers found 1948 a 'blessedly peaceful era' (p.16), a time when farmers could resume their regular lives, relieved that the war had ended.

The Hayden family of Bentrock

David Hayden is the only child of Gail and Wesley Hayden. His Uncle Frank and Aunt Gloria have no children so he has no cousins. His grandparents, Julian and Enid Hayden, now live on their 'dude' ranch outside town. His father has inherited his grandfather's former position of the sheriff of Mercer County and Frank is the town's doctor. This is the extent of the small family around whom the action takes place.

Key point

Here David expresses, for the first time, his disappointment in his father (p.17). In this territory of the Wild West where settlers confronted Indians and 'won' the land, he believes the sheriff should be a more romantic character.

Wesley Hayden is the town sheriff, and is portrayed as being, in both the narrator's and the reader's minds, a caricature of the stereotypical gun-toting, Wild West sheriff who could outshoot a villain at twenty paces. He has a crippled leg and carries out his mundane, routine work unrelieved by excitement. He has only a small rusty, unloaded gun, confiscated and exchanged for a bus ticket out of town. He does not carry a badge because it is too heavy. Later, the significance of the weight of the badge becomes evident; it is symbolic of the weight of the justice which Wesley is unable to administer.

Wesley's loyalty to his father; Marie's illness (pp.19–31)

Key point

David's father is the victim of his own father's power. He is quiet, unambitious and has accepted the position Julian Hayden has thrust upon him; Gail Hayden's ambition for her husband carries less weight.

The narrator's mother, Gail Hayden, has a different background. She has grown up on a prosperous farm in a fertile valley, the opposite of Bentrock, in North Dakota. She is ambitious for David's father who has a law degree and is disappointed as she believes he will only reach his full potential when he gives up his small-town sheriff's job to practise law in a bigger town where his talents would be better appreciated.

Instead, Wesley is expected to carry on the tradition of county sheriff established by his influential father. But he is the opposite of his power-hungry father, Julian Hayden, 'a dominating man who drew sustenance and strength from controlling others' (p.20). He dominates the affairs of Mercer County and in his prime he maintained a large ranch and served unopposed as sheriff.

David's 'wild' side and his mother's views (pp.21–24)

David's mother is also concerned for her son's soul and fears that he is growing up 'wild' (pp.21–22), outside the moral influence of the Lutheran Church. An only child, he is a serious boy not at all influenced by peer group pressures in the town. Indeed, there he feels out of place and seeks escape from the restrictions of classroom and church. He is an outdoors boy, a huntin', shootin', fishin' kind of boy living in the remnants of the Wild West. The land and the Indians are tamed now, but these are an entrenched part of that geography and that social era. But it is more than this. David's solitary nature lends itself to roaming free on his horse

'Nutty'. He is content to 'simply *be*' (p.24) and, at twelve, he starts to explore his inner self.

David, though, is caught up in that model of masculinity that promotes the macho image of war heroes and straight shooters.

Adult narrator

Occasionally, in this early section, the adult David pauses to speak more directly to the reader: 'That was our family in 1948 and those were the tensions that set the air humming in our household' (p.24). Earlier, he has corrected a possible inference by the reader that his mother might seem to be urban and restrictive, which she is not (p.24). This is the first instance of the narrator's obvious respect for and love of his mother in contrast to his disappointment with his father. With the introduction of Marie Little Soldier, which leads into the story proper about her illness, we move into the young David's version of events – see p.27.

David and Marie Little Soldier (pp.24–31)

Marie Little Soldier, a young Indian woman from the nearby reservation, is foregrounded in the real drama, which revolves around her death and the Hayden family. David plays the role of informant to the reader but Marie acts as a catalyst for the action.

In the absence of any close female relatives, David has become close to Marie, the family's housekeeper, who cares for him during the week when his mother is working. Marie, unlike her mother, is not immediately cowed by whites (p.25) and her introduction brings both racial and sexual elements into the story. She is abundant, a kind of earth mother, both physically and in personality:

> close to six feet tall ... a fleshy amplitude ... made her seem simultaneously soft and strong, as if all that body could be ready, at a moment's notice, for sex or work. (p.25)

Young David was close to her in a way not possible even with his mother. His mother's love is underpinned with the need for David to be brought up correctly. She is in charge of his moral and spiritual development whereas Marie is the carer of his physical development and he adores her because she talks to him, is lively and vibrant and because 'she was sexy' although he hastens to add that his love for her was then 'chaste' (p.26).

Ronnie Tall Bear, her boyfriend, is a sporting hero who provides a rare male role model for David and it is through him that David's unconscious awareness of racism surfaces: 'I knew without being told, as if it were knowledge that I drank in with the water, that college was not for Indians' (p.26). In the description of the position of Marie's bedroom, 'a small room off the kitchen' (p.26), David implies that he believes if Marie were not either an Indian or in an inferior position in the household she would have the spare upstairs room.

Marie's illness (pp.27–31)

Key point

Until Marie's death, racism and white supremacy have been issues that have lain dormant, or at least have been ignored under cover of seeming respectability. David's family is plunged into a maelstrom that damages them all.

The action foreshadowed in the Prologue begins. Marie is, uncharacteristically, in her room, coughing. Her illness triggers emotions and prejudices which lie under the surface of seeming normality for David's family and the people of Bentrock. It leads to the discovery of the most heinous crimes: rape, assault, murder and, eventually, suicide.

Marie's feverish condition strips her of all dignity (p.29) but David glimpses her sturdy brown legs and feels a sensual response that reminds him of how he once saw her naked beauty 'just as she was stepping out of the shower' (p.29). In his pre-pubescent state, David is affected both by her strength and her sexuality.

David holds Marie when she coughs (pp.31–33)

Marie's helplessness seems to heighten her sensuality (p.32). David was so moved by the exertions of her coughing that he held 'Marie's shoulders until the coughing subsided ... [and] felt Marie trembling all over' (p.32). Afterwards he found his 'hands ... damp from gripping Marie's shoulders ... Was the sweat mine or hers?' (p.33). Is this because of his extreme anxiety over Marie's illness? Or has his physical contact with Marie stirred not only his sensuality but also his sexuality? Is the adult narrator now recognising his younger self's innocent arousal?

Young David's role in the novel (p.30)

The twelve-year-old David's role as eavesdropper/narrator/informant is established here (p.30). While ostensibly waiting outside Marie's room, David not only hears his mother's interrogation of the sick woman, but also intervenes and acts on what he hears. This sets the pattern of behaviour for the young David/narrator whose later observances lead to a charge of murder against his Uncle Frank.

Marie's reaction to Frank (pp.33–35)

Inexplicably, Marie's illness is intensified by her obvious anxiety about seeing the doctor. Uncle Frank is not only Wesley's brother, but also the town's respected medical practitioner. Gail Hayden thinks that Marie is worried about the expense and reassures her that there will be no charge. When David reiterates Marie's objections, Wes Hayden thinks it is because she is an ignorant Indian, used only to the superstitious treatments of the medicine man.

David learns about racism (pp.34–35)

David realises he cannot shut out what has already been heard/learned. He admits he wants to forget his father's, and his community's, racial prejudice but he has to acknowledge his father's dislike of Indians (p.34). It is not a personal dislike, but something worse, a contempt reflecting his upbringing and community attitudes:

> He simply held them in low regard ... he believed Indians, with only a few exceptions, were ignorant, lazy, superstitious, and irresponsible. (p.34)

David recalls his first awareness of this kind of prejudice when, at eight, his father forbade him to wear a pair of moccasins given to him as a present. If he wore them he'd become 'as flat-footed and lazy as an Indian' (p.34).

When David's father labels Marie's refusal to see Uncle Frank as 'Indian superstition', David withholds further protests to avoid his father's 'scorching sarcasm' (p.34). Wesley rings his sister-in-law, Gloria, to ask her to send Frank to attend Marie.

The entrenched nature of racism is epitomised by the banter between Wes and Frank. Wes reiterates his opinion that Marie has only ever been to a medicine man while Frank offers 'to do a little dance around the bed' and 'try beating some drums' (p.35). Both find this exchange amusing but David's mother 'didn't laugh'. She is aware of the seriousness of Marie's illness and her distress at the doctor being called, as well as the overt racism.

Aunt Gloria (pp.34–35)

David reveals that he holds Aunt Gloria's beauty (she is small and blonde) in such high regard that he thinks she is even 'prettier than [his] mother ... a significant admission for a boy to make' (p.35). But she and Frank have no children, a circumstance which makes her the butt of unpleasant speculation between David's grandfather and Frank (p.35). However, this really only suggests that Frank is barren, symbolic of his moral state.

Wesley and Frank contrasted (pp.35–38)

Key point

At Frank's entrance, David contrasts the brothers at the expense of his own father (pp.35–38). Frank is everything Wesley is not.

Frank possesses an 'athletic grace', is a war hero, a doctor. Wesley has a crippled knee, was unfit for war and is merely the town sheriff, his law degree neglected in favour of loyalty to carrying on his father's occupation, although he never sought or assumed the power in the community that his father exercises. The 'stolid … steady and dependable' Wesley seems, in every way, inferior to his 'witty, charming' (p.36) brother. The reader assumes that Wesley is the older of the two brothers but this is not made clear. If so, even the role of leader has been reversed for Frank seems to be the natural leader.

However, Wesley possesses one capacity that his brother does not: a possibility that he can develop both morally and spiritually. Frank's veneer of 'charm', and that he is very much his father's son, stand in the way of his attaining any kind of self-awareness. He basks in the sun of his father's, and the town's, approval and the kind of power that Julian exercises corrupts Frank. Nevertheless, David finds his father 'inescapably dull' in comparison. 'Nothing glittered in my father's wake the way it did in Uncle Frank's' (p.36). The saying 'all that glitters is not gold' springs to mind, for Frank is superficial and without honour.

The shallowness of Frank is reinforced by the performance of David's grandfather, Julian Hayden, at the celebratory picnic for returned soldiers, which David recalls. His commanding presence dominates both the occasion and those gathered there: 'He didn't call for silence … He assumed that once people saw him, they would give him their attention. And they did' (p.37).

And to the father of Frank and Wesley there is only one son, only one to be proud of and to exalt. Wesley merges with the crowd, collecting scraps of paper from the grass, a suitably humble occupation for the other son. David is profoundly affected by this contrasting treatment that all accept as normal and only he seems to question simply by noticing (p.38).

Julian Hayden's power

It is interesting to note here that Julian Hayden has not yet formally entered centre stage in the novel and yet the reader is profoundly aware of his presence behind the action so far. David, like everyone else in the story, is affected by his grandfather's power. Even behind the brothers' chitchat about erecting a fence, David 'wondered what Grandpa Hayden would say' as 'he still had the nineteenth-century cattleman's open range mentality and hatred of fences' (p.39). Frank is prepared to risk his father's anger but Wesley is loyal to his father's ideal and 'refused to put up a fence as all [the] neighbours had' (p.39).

Frank visits Marie Little Soldier (pp.38–49)

Frank enters Marie's room and shuts the door. Marie screams anxiously for Gail and Frank reluctantly allows her in. David, in the role of eavesdropper, manoeuvres himself into an advantageous position. Soon he heard '– muffled but unmistakable – Marie shout another *no*' (p.41).

Being a woman compounds the problem of prejudice against the Indians. In Montana in 1948 'women's rights' were unheard of except for the courtesies extended to 'ladies' such as 'no swearing in front of my mother' (p.40). Frank does not even leave the door open for Marie's peace of mind when he knows of her reluctance to see a doctor. It does not occur to him that Gail Hayden should be present at her examination, despite Marie's obvious distress.

Marie's screams alert David to something untoward between his uncle and Marie. However, what prompts a boy leading such a sheltered life to think, 'After what had just happened with Marie I didn't want to be alone with Uncle Frank' (p.41)? There is no apparent or imagined threat to him.

Typically, David's father pretends to ignore the drama happening in Marie's room. He does ask his brother, 'What was the problem with Marie?' (p.42) but is reassured when Frank panders to his racist view: 'They're used to being treated by the medicine man. Or some old squaw. But a doctor comes around and they think he's the evil spirit or something' (p.42). The reader knows Frank is lying at this point as Marie has declared earlier that she usually sees the same white doctor as Gail Hayden, Dr. Snow. Wesley retreats into the comfort of a nineteenth-century platitude: 'They're not going to make it into the twentieth century until they give up their superstitions and old ways' (p.42). The irony that 1948 is already halfway through the twentieth century seems to escape him.

Gail Hayden reveals Frank's sexual crimes (pp.38–49)

Frank appears to be concerned about the Indians' welfare but David senses that it is not Marie's pneumonia that is the problem. His mother has been in the room with Marie and her shocked responses confirm David's sense of foreboding: 'she held her hands to her mouth ... her attitude was exactly like someone who has seen something frightening' (pp.42–43).

Gail supports Marie

Key point

Gail learns from Marie that Frank has committed sexual crimes against defenceless Indian girls and women and insists on pressing for justice on their behalf. Gail's determination changes all of their lives forever.

Gail has been portrayed as an honest, intelligent woman, a woman of her times who defers to her husband but who nurtures David's moral and spiritual development. She knows that rape and sexual assault against Indian girls is as reprehensible as against white girls. It is her duty to convince her husband that Frank's behaviour is criminal. On behalf of Marie she becomes unnaturally assertive towards Frank and Wesley. She insists that Marie will stay in her care where 'we can keep an eye on her' (p.43). Her anger is barely concealed and David is puzzled at its source, yet realises, because of Frank's abrupt departure, that it has something to do with him.

Gail insists that Wesley listen, in private, to what she has discovered. She is so enraged about women from a minority group being molested by a white man in a position of trust and authority, her tone commands Wes's attention. As she recounts what has been happening, her assurance grows and it is the overcoming of her disinclination to use basic sexual terms like 'Rape. Breasts. Penis' (pp.47–48), which finally convinces Wesley that there is a problem which must be addressed. Characteristically, he wishes she had not 'told the sheriff' (p.48).

David gains adult awareness

Key point

Twelve-year-old David's narrator role crystallises here as the quintessential eavesdropper who now does not merely overhear chance remarks but actively seeks to hear, and understand, his uncle's part in the drama. As a consequence, 'charming, affable Uncle Frank' is 'gone for good'.

For David, the transition for the child from innocence to an adult awareness is expressed in a formative moment of realisation:

> If I had gone back into the house ... I would never have heard the conversation between my father and mother, and perhaps I would have lived out my life with an illusion about my family and perhaps even the human community. (pp.44–45)

The narrator frames his mother's revelations with a picture of nature's peace and harmony: his 'mother's hollyhocks and snapdragons ... and the bees that flew in and out of the flowers [filling] the air with their drone' (p.45). This contrasts starkly with the disclosures of abnormal nature which are to follow and marks the end of peace for David and his family.

Just before this climax, Frank's personal charm has been underlined, but then undermined. Gail suspects that charm is used to hide 'some personal deficit or lack of substance. If your character was sound, you didn't need charm' (p.44). The revelations about Frank's character now lend weight to her accusations against him. Her husband cannot doubt her story and David knows that 'Charming, affable Uncle Frank was gone for good' (p.49).

The McAuleys (pp.50–51)

The Deputy Sheriff, Len McAuley, is introduced after Marie has been interrogated by the sheriff (p.50). He bridges the regimes of both grandfather and father as sheriff. David has the kind of affection for Len and his wife Daisy usually reserved for grandparents but David's own grandparents are far removed in nature from this closeness.

David tries to eavesdrop on two parallel conversations: that between his father and the Deputy and that between his mother and the rather garrulous Daisy. The point of interest of both conversations is Marie Little Soldier and Daisy confirms that there is substance to Marie's allegations against Frank (p.51).

David's perceptions irrevocably changed (pp.51–54)

David, now present throughout his parents' conversation, understands that the disclosures about his Uncle Frank have inevitably damaged both his mother's and his own regard for his father:

> Then I knew. She saw him now as she hadn't before. He was not only her husband, he was a *brother*, and brother to a man who used his profession to take advantage of women, brother to a *pervert!* (p.52)

The reader cannot really know his mother's thoughts any more than David can, but the declaration that David shares his mother's thoughts has an aura of authenticity about it and marks significant changes in both his mother's attitudes and David's awareness of adult relationships.

Key point

David also begins to comprehend that his father's fidelity to his grandfather's quest for all-consuming power is a kind of moral corruption.

When Wesley says, 'I don't want this getting back to my father', David suddenly understands:

> *That* was what my father believed in. If he could not sufficiently fear, love, trust obey and honor God ... it was because he had nothing left for his Heavenly Father after declaring absolute fealty to his earthly one. (p.53)

It is this misplaced loyalty which stands in the way of justice and it is David's father's moral dilemma at the end of Part One which becomes the central focus of the novel. Wesley Hayden knows that his brother is guilty of raping defenceless girls: 'my father knew him as well as any man or woman' (p.54). His allegiance to the power of his own father is set against his allegiance to upholding the law.

David waits breathlessly to hear his father say that he doesn't believe that Frank sexually abuses Indian women – but Wes's silence condemns him and David can no longer ignore the truth: 'my father knew [Frank] was guilty' (p.54).

Part Two (pp.57–102)

Investigation into Frank Hayden's crimes (pp.57–61)

David deduces that his father has begun investigating Marie's allegations, first because he goes to the Indian reservation on the pretext of buying honey and second because later in the local diner, Coffee Cup, he does not sit with his usual cronies. Instead, he is with a respected leader of the Indian community, Ollie Young Bear, an Indian Wesley Hayden particularly admires for his 'white' lifestyle but whom David dislikes. He is probably the last person who would know about the molestation of Indian girls by a white doctor as he has 'no special status among the Indians' (p.60). When David approaches the pair in the diner, he is not welcome and can glean no information about Marie's case.

An ominous silence in the house (pp.61–62)

David returns home to find Marie sleeping, but he feels something is wrong. 'It was the silence' (p.61). This is the first time that Watson uses the motif of 'silence' to create atmosphere and to enhance the suspense.

The silence is relieved when David turns the radio on to the Big Band music, which Marie loves and which will always remind him of her.

Wesley interviews Marie (pp.62–66)

Wesley wishes to interview Marie again, following his visit to the reservation and his conversation with Ollie Young Bear. David and his mother are excluded, but David suspects that he has dual motives for wanting to be alone with Marie: either to spare his wife from the sordid details of Frank's behaviour, or to protect his brother.

David's desire to be included as an adult (pp.63–66)

David has a burning desire to be included in the 'family business' for he wants 'adult status' (p.64). Alone with his mother, he hesitates for he doesn't want to hear about anything nasty. When he plucks up courage and asks directly, Gail is evasive and talks about 'wind and dirt and childhood' (p.65). The adult narrator notes that had he had any sensitivity at all, he would have realised that his mother 'wanted a few moments of purity, a temporary escape from the sordid drama' (p.65). His mother might also want him to retain his own childhood innocence, but David 'was on the trail that would lead [him] out of childhood' (p.65).

David's family visit grandfather's ranch (pp.66–73)

When David's grandparents, in particular, his grandfather, are finally directly introduced in Part Two, readers already know what type of man he is. There is a tense silence between David's parents as they drive towards the Hayden ranch, as his mother does not want to be in Frank's company.

The house David's grandfather has built on his 'dude' ranch is huge and loudly proclaims his wealth and status. It dominates the landscape just as his grandfather dominates the community (p.68). David, however, loves the house for its spaciousness.

Julian Hayden is a towering figure whom David imagines is speculating about how he can protect 'his beloved son' (p.69) so he lingers behind a screen door in order to hear the initial exchange between his father and his grandfather 'about Frank' (p.71).

Julian confirms Frank's guilt and his own (pp.71–73)

David naively believes that his grandfather is so powerful 'he'll take care of everything ... He'll shake him up and shout in Frank's face that he'd better straighten up and fly right' (p.71). However, rather than confront Julian about Frank's crimes, David's father weakly turns his attention to

Frank's lack of children. There is an implication here that Julian's nagging about Frank's barrenness has contributed to his sexual crimes.

Julian Hayden's coarseness is emphasised here when he says Gloria has 'enough tit for twins' (p.71). David is shocked, not only by this remark, but also by the revelations which follow. Julian wants more than one grandchild and he wants 'them white' (p.72). That short remark implicates Julian in a conspiracy of knowledge about Frank's crimes against Indian girls. It implies, of course, that Frank is merely following Julian's own example of being 'partial to red meat' (p.72). Even worse is the allusion to Wesley, himself, already knowing about Frank's boyhood sexual initiation with 'that little Indian girl' (p.72) and that already he enjoyed exerting his power over others: 'He had that little squaw down on her hands and knees' (p.72). Julian's obvious amusement at this is even more shocking. This evidence supports Marie's story of Frank's depravity and the next remark cements the evidence that Frank's sexual activities were in the full knowledge, and approval, of his father: 'I wouldn't be surprised if there wasn't some young ones out on the reservation who look a lot like your brother' (p.72).

David's eavesdropping escapes detection but prompts the following recollection of the earlier incident when Julian spoke of Frank and Indian girls.

Frank and Gloria's wedding (pp.73–76)

For Frank and Gloria's wedding the Hayden family had travelled to Minneapolis, Minnesota. David recalls his father attending Frank's bucks' night where Wesley had become extremely drunk and his grandfather had acted like a typical cowboy, the narrator reinforcing for the reader the natures of Julian Hayden and his sons. On the train journey home after the wedding grandfather alluded to Frank's proclivities: 'Now he's got himself a good-looking white woman for a wife. That better keep him off the reservation' (p.76). David recalls the family's silence – no one dared challenge Julian or criticise Frank.

David's sexuality and new self-awareness (pp.76–82)

Key point

This crucial section shows David's burgeoning sexuality in relation to Aunt Gloria, his increased understanding of adult relationships, and his own understanding of life's complexities when he shoots the magpie.

Enid Hayden, David's grandmother, is a nervous, quiet woman, her own personality subsumed under her husband's many years before. David thinks she is a 'pathetic' figure (p.76). He has no appetite for lunch and wonders how the 'sweet and beautiful' Gloria could 'act normal … How could she not know' (p.77) what Frank is guilty of?

David's sexual feelings for Gloria

It is here that the reader learns of David's sexual stirrings. He fears his thoughts are not 'the cleanest' but leaves the reader to imagine what his fantasies about Gloria are, prompted by his 'own desire. I thought Aunt Gloria was more than pretty' (p.77).

A year before Gloria had nursed him through a bout of tonsillitis. When she came in one night to check on him, she aroused him sexually when he smelt her perfume and saw her breasts silhouetted perfectly in soft light (pp.77–78).

David feels ashamed for having such feelings. That he is at the threshold of puberty is clear as he listens to the lovemaking of Frank and Gloria through the wall (p.78), and is jealous of Uncle Frank.

At dinner that Sunday, however, 'It was shame again' (p.78) that kept his eyes down, but Aunt Gloria's 'lush sweet floral scent … did not excite me this time. This time it made me so sad I wanted to cry' (p.78). Why? Does he recognise Frank's sexual betrayal of the innocent and lovely Gloria? Does his knowledge of adult behaviour now let him see beneath apparent surface happiness?

David shoots the magpie (pp.80–82)

This moment leads to another formative experience for David who escapes after the family dinner. His grandfather gives him a handgun and some ammunition and encourages him to go out and 'blast' coyotes. David's other guns are single shot, so this is a novelty for him. Shooting is a normal activity for a boy in Montana in 1948 but instead of taking the opportunity to improve his marksmanship, David uses the 'entire box of bullets' (p.80) in random shooting. Clearly this is an outlet for David's disturbed thoughts about Gloria, Uncle Frank, his own father and his grandfather. His parents have no idea that David has grasped the significance of what is happening around him, believing him still to be an innocent boy, unmoved yet by his own sexuality and not expecting him to understand the complexities of racism or of Frank's sinful predilection for Indian girls. David is endeavouring to sift through the maze that has suddenly revealed the complexities of adulthood.

Sex, violence and death

His disquiet is reflected in his killing of a magpie, a random kill among all the missed, hasty shots. When he sees 'its half-open, glassy green eye … already beginning to dust over' (p.81), David feels something beyond his usual extraordinary feelings of 'power and sadness, exhilaration and fear' (p.81). He has killed before but now he 'felt strangely calm'. He had not known it, but he 'needed to kill something' (p.81) to release his pent-up emotions. For David, growing up in the Wild West, guns are a part of the culture and to kill is macho. This need to kill releases other thoughts that show his emerging self-awareness and the knowledge that contradictions are part of the complexity of human life.

> I realized that these strange, unthought-of connections – sex and death, lust and violence, desire and degradation – are there, deep in even a good heart's chambers. (p.82)

He, too, is human and holds within himself these same complexities. These emotions are a part of the other side of love and life, a mature perspective that David can now bring to bear on the rest of the events of that summer. But this killing also shows that David now links sexuality with death and violence, even if it is at an unconscious or subconscious level.

Wesley and Frank – blood brothers (pp.82–84)

On his way back David sees his father and Uncle Frank arguing angrily. From high up he notices for the first time 'how the two men were brothers in posture and attitude' (p.83). Instead of accentuating their differences as he has done formerly, David suddenly realises their similarities and the fact that bloodlines count. They are obviously arguing over Marie's accusations and Frank moves threateningly towards David's father. In that moment David takes out his unloaded gun and points it towards Frank. His intentions are unclear, even to himself, but the situation presents itself as one way of solving everyone's problems:

> my first question wasn't, could I pull the trigger; it was, could I hit my target. Only after ... did I wonder what might happen if I killed my uncle ... Could I get away with it? (p.84)

David is plunged, by his own actions, into an adult dilemma. First, he realises that, given the opportunity, men will kill. He has already proved that by the afternoon's shooting. Second, he wonders what such a killing would prove and, third, his instinct for self-preservation surfaces. He is relieved that he has avoided the moment as the brothers walk off together.

The sheriff decides to take no action (pp.84–85)

Wesley will do nothing about Frank's criminal behaviour and the damage already done because Frank has promised his brother that 'he's going to cut it out' (p.85). But David's mother is distraught: 'Sins – crimes – are not supposed to go unpunished' (p.85). For her it is a matter of justice. For the sheriff the damage 'can't be undone ... That's over and done' (p.85). This justifies his decision not to act.

Community attitudes

Is Wesley just weak? In the Montana of 1948 the community is intent on peace after the war and they do not want that peace disturbed by raking over matters that were then considered trivial. The prevailing racist attitudes underpin the behaviour of the citizens and in a community dominated by Julian Hayden, a white doctor's fornication with girls on the reservation would be overlooked or ignored. After reading the Epilogue of the novel, the reader may conclude that this was probably the only effective course of action. Through Gail's voice though, this inertia is examined and found wanting. The novel remains true to the period as Gail fails in her quest. Given subsequent events, it would appear that Frank has not been convinced of Wesley's intended lack of action against him.

Marie asks about coyotes (pp.85–86)

At home, Marie is feeling stronger and on the way to recovery. Is her reference to David's inability to see a coyote (p.86) meant to be an enigmatic reference to the human inability to tell the good guys from the bad? Are both Frank and Wesley coyotes? Are both wily and manipulative? Are truth and justice inextricably linked or are these cornerstones of civilisation elusive and often disguised? Or does Marie have some prescient feeling about what is to overtake both her and the family?

Marie's death (pp.86–91)

Next day when David returned home from fishing with a friend, Marie is dead. When he saw the hearse outside his house he knew 'immediately what had happened' (p.87). And for him, 'all usual activity ... ceased' (p.87). He considered walking past his house and walking on forever out of Bentrock, away from his childhood, walking until he could find 'a place where [he] could bury that secret forever' (p.87).

David's growing maturity

It is part of his growing maturity that he realises that no such place exists, that there can be no avoidance of reality. At this point the motif of light recurs. When David sees his uncle filling out the Certificate of Death, he sees his black bag in a supernatural way; he imagines that 'if its black mouth opened, it could swallow all the light in the room' (p.87). If light here represents truth and justice, then certainly it has been swallowed at that moment.

Responses to Marie's death

David's mother is slumped over, her fingers drumming on the table in a frantic activity, which belies her posture. Her embrace of David is to seek comfort for herself rather than to offer him consolation.

Frank assures everyone that Marie, despite reports of her recovery, has suffered a 'sudden relapse' (p.88).

David, however, knows otherwise but tries to deny it by blaming the smell of fish as the thing that makes him seem the odd one out in the room. 'It was that and not the secret I held, the fearful knowledge' (p.88). David is also repelled that everyone else goes through the rituals associated with death.

Wesley is unable to contact Marie's relatives and decides to drive out to the reservation to notify them. David contemplates whether it would be better to accompany his father 'and tell him' what he knew (p.90), but he knows he cannot face the grief his father's visit will engender. It is then that he also recognises, with a new maturity, the less glamorous but more difficult side of his father's job, the sheriff as bearer of bad news.

Daisy, the Deputy Sheriff's wife, recognises Gail's incomprehension at Marie's death and that she feels responsible so she sends David across to her house.

Deputy Sheriff bridges two generations of justice (pp.91–95)

The Deputy's house is in darkness with only pinpoints of light, perhaps symbolic of Len McAuley's darkness of the spirit. For years his position as Julian Hayden's deputy has meant that he has had to stand by while ideals of justice have been compromised in Bentrock. He must have known, just as Julian Hayden did, that Frank has been frequenting the Indian reservation for sex with the Indian girls and, given Julian Hayden's domination, there must have been other compromises of justice. It is implied that this is why Len became an alcoholic. The community was relieved when Len 'quit drinking' (p.92). That Len now has a glass of whisky in front of him signifies to David the gravity of the situation: 'I felt as bad seeing that glass of whiskey as I had when I'd first heard Marie cough' (p.92).

Nature of justice under Julian Hayden

Here, again, the motif of 'silence' underlines the significance of Marie's death and the burden of knowledge that the Deputy has carried. In bridging the regimes of Julian and Wesley as sheriffs, Len has walked a fine line. His duty is to support the sheriff, not to make his own decisions. Now he tries to explain to David the delicacy of maintaining peace in Mercer County which does not always have anything to do with justice: 'your granddad said it means ... knowing when to look and when to look away' (p.93). As it took him a while to realise that, he adds for David's benefit: 'Your dad hasn't quite got the hang of it. Not just yet' (p.93).

Whether Wesley is ever to get 'the hang of it' becomes one of the focal points of the novel, for it is how he deals with the consequences of Marie's death that affects them all.

Does Len know about Marie's death?

David thinks Len is 'hallucinating' under the influence of the whisky but then he provides some enlightenment for David about the circumstances leading up to the present predicament in which his father finds himself. Len wanted to tell Julian Hayden to 'rein' his boys in, not to let them run wild just because they were 'a thousand miles from nowhere ... But [he] didn't. Never said a word. Now look at them' (p.94).

Len feels partly responsible for the misfortunes overtaking the family. David is not sure whether Len is just rambling, but the reader knows that he is trying to tell David that he, too, knows what happened to Marie because he is only 'feigning repose and inattention' (p.93). He is, in fact, trying to give David an opening for telling what he knows, which David glimpses: 'something parted, as if the wind blew a curtain open and allowed a flash of sunlight into the room. Did Len know what I knew?' (p.94).

Light, again, recurs as a motif to heighten the moment of illumination but David is not sure that Len is 'talking about the same thing' (p.94). Len knows the moment is lost but urges David to look after his mother (p.94). David then wonders if this is a further adult complication – perhaps Len is in love with his mother. He recalls all the little chores he does for her and particularly 'the way he removed his hat when he came into our house and fiddled with it, creasing and denting the crown, running his finger around the sweatband' (pp.94–5). With his maturing awareness of his own sexuality, is he now able to recognise sexual attraction between others? He concludes that if Len does love his mother, then 'Why not say [Len's] was one more heart broken in this sequence of events?' (p.95). Is David's innocence being snatched from him too quickly in his new knowledge of adult behaviour?

David reveals that Frank saw Marie the day she died (pp.95–100)

David is so burdened with what he has seen that in the night he feels 'death' in the house (p.95). He is so afraid of the supernatural visions he has conjured up that he seeks comfort from his parents. He explains to his father that, on the fateful day of Marie's death, he saw Uncle Frank leave their house at about three o'clock, carrying his medical bag (p.96).

Wesley's response

His mother realises the implication of David's story but his father adopts his sheriff persona and becomes his interrogator. The brother in him does not want to believe the obvious conclusion that Frank has murdered Marie. He thinks that if only David had seen Frank, then it could all be covered up. Wesley does not realise that David is no longer the child he was before; he is now capable of manipulating events in his new knowledge of Frank's crimes. He reveals his suspicion that Len has also seen Frank leaving the house (p.99).

For Wesley this is a catastrophe because Len holds the unique position of intimately knowing the family and its weaknesses. He knows that Len will say nothing but that his look will be one of reproach: 'There he'll be, day after day. With that look. I'm not going to live with that look' (p.100).

David becomes acutely aware of his father's daily physical pain and equates that with the emotional pain he now feels over his brother. He also realises that his father harbours 'both jealousy and resentment' (p.100) that he, alone, must carry the burden of resolving the matter.

Up to this point Wesley has not undergone any moral development, and now if he seeks justice for Marie's death it is only because someone else knows about it.

End of Part Two – David's vision of Indians (pp.101–102)

David reflects on the Indians of Bentrock that evening in bed. He recognises that they are a dispossessed people, 'objects of the most patronizing and debilitating prejudice ... a largely passive and benign presence' (p.101). David, influenced by all the cowboy and Indian films he has seen, and by the legends of his own neighbourhood, dreams that all the Indians from the reservation and the region around gather on nearby Circle Hill to do avenge Marie's death. However, they are not in warrior mode, but peacefully demonstrating. They are no longer the proud, free-roaming custodians of the plains; they are a disempowered minority group incapable of taking action against the abusers of their race.

Part Three (pp.105–162)

Wesley tries to preserve the family honour (pp.105–106)

Marie is buried in a neighbouring state away from the scene of her death. David's father is working very hard gaining support 'by gathering in friends and favors' (p.106). David recognises that this is the pattern pursued when his father is closing in on a suspect: 'rather than become grim and dogged my father became good-humored and gregarious. He became charming' (p.106). And, the irony not escaping David, 'He became more like his brother' (p.106).

Wesley hides Frank in the basement (pp.107–114)

Wesley's way of resolving the situation is not to seek justice openly but to conceal the matter and so he physically hides Frank in their own basement without charging him with any crime. David and Gail are horrified, both wanting to see Frank brought to justice openly. Wesley is troubled, not by the fact that Frank has murdered Marie, but because he has to preserve the family's honour. For him locking up his brother is a traumatic occurrence and he retreats into silence until Gail returns. David has a lurid turn of mind, believing that his father, in his weakness, has killed Frank in the basement as a way 'to bring his brother to justice for his crimes' (p.109). The reality is not as shocking: Wesley insists on secrecy as no one else knows, but Gail insists that Gloria be told the truth, and not just 'that Frank's in some trouble' (p.111). Frank himself acts 'as if this is all some kind of joke' (p.111).

Painting the house – Gail's civilising influence (pp.112–113)

As his father leaves to tell Gloria, he calls David and creates a metaphor for him using the painting of the house. It must be scraped and sanded and covered with two coats of white paint. This is the hard work associated with bringing Frank to justice urged by his wife and by his duty to carry out the law. He makes it quite clear with this metaphor that if it were up to him, he would 'let every house in town go' (p.113), just as he would let Frank go. It is 'Paint ... That's how you find life and civilization. Women come and they want fresh paint' (p.113). It is apparent that Gail is the civilising influence on him and that left to himself he would be more like his father, more like Frank. Perhaps, too, Wesley's knowledge that he has to fight Julian makes him reluctant to uphold the law.

David given responsibility

He warns David that if there is any trouble he is to fetch Len from across the road. Clearly, Wesley is expecting trouble from his own father who will not give up his beloved son to justice over the matter of a mere Indian woman.

Julian and Enid Hayden visit (pp.114–125)

David's grandparents arrive, inevitably, to demand Frank's release. Bombastically, Julian insists, 'Bring him out here ... Now. Right goddam now' (p.115). And as if no one heard: 'Wesley ... Get your ass in gear and get your brother out here now' (p.115). Like the reader, David wonders how his father can withstand such overbearing demands and what it must have been like 'to have a father capable of speaking to you like that' (p.116).

Wesley tries to point out that this 'isn't about family', that it is 'a legal matter' (p.116), but his assertions are swept aside. Eventually, as Julian Hayden lights up a cigar, David is sent upstairs. Although glad to leave, he has no intention of missing the drama so he hurries to the spare room to listen through a vent.

Julian Hayden asserts his authority

Wesley endeavours to proceed with a rational discussion but his father's overt racist attitude prevents him from understanding the gravity of the situation. The only way Julian can rationalise the arrest of Frank is to tell himself that Wesley is jealous of his brother and that he has locked him up as an act of revenge. Julian has nothing but contempt for Wesley: 'You – *investigating*?' (p.118) is his sarcastic retort to Wesley's statement that Frank has been arrested for 'taking liberties with ... his Indian patients"' (p.118). He speaks to Wesley with loathing:

> Now you pull a fucking stunt like this. I should've taken you aside and got you straightened out. If it meant whipping your ass I should've got you straightened out. (p.119)

Even when Wesley is pushed to tell them Frank has committed murder, Julian still thinks he can control the situation and stop it all (p.122).

David's responses (p.122)

Julian's anger profoundly affects David, and when his father says: 'This has to go its own way' (p.122) he recalls how he could have shot Frank and resolved the matter forever. After his grandparents leave, David feels apprehensive, afraid even of being with his parents. The air is so full of anger and anguish that he realises 'it seemed unwise to depend on anyone' (p.122). He decides it is safer to remain in the bedroom: his world has shifted and he feels there is no safe place for him.

David learns about human mortality

David, though, is still a boy and the thought of chocolate cake entices him downstairs. There he is met with the sight of his parents in a scene of tenderness. The stress of the confrontation with Julian, and the anguish over what he must do with his brother, has been too much for David's father who has been crying (p.122). David, shocked by how 'old' his father looks, is confronted with the realisation that his father will 'die someday' (p.124).

David desperately needs some reassurance and yearns for his parents to interpret all the raw knowledge for him, 'to explain it so it wasn't as bad as the facts made it seem' (p.124). His father is so immersed in his own role that he fails to see the effect it is having on his son and instead tells David not to let his grandfather or grandmother into the house if no one else is at home.

David cries for Nutty (p.125)

This added responsibility is too much for David. He cries, not for himself or for the people involved in the situation, but for his horse. He believes that now he will never see Nutty again if his family is estranged from his grandparents. He comes to the philosophical conclusion that 'Now the distance between us seemed too great for either Nutty or me to travel ever again' (p.125). This reference is a metaphorical one. The distance is how far David has travelled from innocence to experience rather than distance in miles. For he can never again be the boy who rode carefree around his grandfather's ranch.

The Hayden name; David's sexual shame (pp.125–130)

The Hayden family have always been leaders of their community and David realises that this has given him unearned advantages. He concludes now that when the scandal of Uncle Frank becomes known, he will also be tarred with the brush of disgrace, also undeserved. The community of Bentrock has tolerated all kinds of eccentricities, but David senses that this scandal will not be overlooked.

As he walks down the main street, he starts to imagine what his uncle may have done that was criminal to all his female patients from his ex-teacher to a high-school girl. To his dismay, thinking about what might have happened to Loretta Waterman arouses David sexually (p.129). He cannot ignore his adolescence, but puberty now seems to be aligned with shame and disgust. Here his lack of appropriate male role models is beginning to leave its mark. He has not been given any positive reinforcement about his masculinity – it seems to him to be associated with perversion. His knowledge of sexual abuse becomes a heavy burden for David and damages his adult perspective of love and sex. In the Epilogue, the reader learns that the adult David has never revealed these terrible, formative events to his wife, indicating the extent of the damage to him.

Is it a good idea to pursue justice?

Here David also notes that Montana in 1948 seemed to tolerate all sorts of behaviour, 'from the eccentric to the unusual to the aberrant', including his uncle Frank who 'molested his patients' (p.128). He is now not so sure that bringing Frank to justice will be a good thing. Perhaps it would be easier to just let him go, as his father would rather do because the shame being brought on the family is too much for him and he asks, 'what's it all for?' (p.129). His mother assures him that bringing Frank to justice is the proper course, but David observes that 'we're the ones getting the shitty end of the stick' (p.130), that it is having more effect on his family than on Frank or his grandfather. His mother admits that he 'might be right' (p.130).

Julian attempts to release Frank (pp.130–151)

As Wesley had expected, Julian takes action to secure the release of his son. He sends his workers in a truck to facilitate Frank's escape from the basement. In what seems like the enactment of a scene from a Western movie, Julian's men 'walk abreast of each other but spaced out so that together they took up almost the entire width of the yard' (p.133). David tries to contact his father or Len, but fails. His mother takes up the challenge with Wesley's shotgun ready to defend not just her home, but the honour of the sheriff.

David is moved by her vulnerability and tries to assume the role of adult male, but his mother knows he is not yet ready for that and sends him away to find '*someone*' to help. He rushes around searching unsuccessfully until 'the shotgun boomed' (p.136). David is momentarily breathless:

> its blast was so loud, so wrongly out of place along that quiet, tree-lined, middle-class American street that the air itself seemed instantly altered, turned foul. (pp.136–137)

David sees this is only a warning shot, but his greatest fear is that his mother will actually shoot someone and he is desperate to stop her, 'to protect her ... from herself and the life she'd have to lead with someone's blood on her hands' (p.138).

Their saviour comes in the form of a dishevelled Len McAuley, armed with a gun aimed at the four intruders. The men retreat. The motif of light recurs here as a contrast to the drama just enacted:

> The sun was shining; an unremarkable fact except that I felt, standing on our lawn, as if I had just returned from a strange, hostile country where there was neither sunlight nor soft grass. (p.139)

Indeed, this is precisely the country which Bentrock will become for the family.

Betrayal and loyalty

David's mother embraces Len for having come to their aid and indicates that David should join her. Momentarily, David imagines a 'new family consisting of Len our protector, my mother, and me' (p.140). This arouses in him thoughts of 'betrayal and loyalty', the very nub of his father's dilemma: just for a second, David has been put in his father's place.

His father arrives, slow because of his injured leg, and this late arrival underlines his impotency. This is further emphasised when he admits that the only charge that can be laid against Frank is for sexual assault – there is 'No chance of an indictment' for Marie's murder (p.141).

David's insights into personal responsibility

David realises that he is beginning to be admitted to adulthood when his father uses the word 'sexual' (p.141) in front of him, and this new maturity is acknowledged when he realises that his father is apologetic for matters out of his control. David recognises that it is not his fault that Julian's men came, that he is Frank's brother or Julian's son and that he lives in Montana, not in Minneapolis as 'an attorney' (p.142); he sees that individuals are 'not responsible for the circumstances of [their] birth or the sins of [their] fathers' (p.142).

Gail urges Wesley to release Frank on the grounds of her family's safety. The reader probably concurs. For if Frank cannot be made responsible for murder, then the lesser charge is not worth pursuing if the family is to be endangered (p.143).

Loyalty and moral absolutism

Len agrees that proving the charge of sexual assault will be difficult and that keeping Frank in the basement will encourage Julian Hayden to try again to release him. Furthermore, in the forthcoming election for the sheriff's position, everyone who holds allegiance to Julian will oppose Wesley.

David is now present for the exchange between the three adults; they make no move to shield him. His mother seems to have abandoned the role of moral protector and admits, 'There was no point in protecting [children] from words when evil and danger were so near at hand' (p.147).

Wesley descends to the basement to release his brother. Although David feels unable to face his uncle, he remains 'out of loyalty' (p.149), now more able to appreciate the complex issues facing his father and the problems of moral certainty.

Frank confesses to Marie's murder (pp.149–150)

Frank confesses to Marie's murder, almost as though he is intent on a kind of warped revenge against Wesley, inexplicable to either the reader or to David.

The sheriff is thrust into a position where he must now uphold the law because his brother's crime is so heinous that he declares vehemently, 'I can't let him loose. Not and live with myself' (p.150) and Gail thinks that Marie's death must have been more horrible than she can imagine.

David is acutely aware of the role each parent has played in the drama and now observes that his 'parents' usual roles had neatly reversed themselves. My mother now represented practicality and expediency; my father stood for moral absolutism' (p.150). No one now, not even his wife, can relieve Wesley's suffering and David realises that there is such a gulf between each of them that they cannot reach out to each other.

Frank smashes the jars (pp.151–154)

Gail's stock of preserves is in the basement and during the night, 'the jars began to break' (p.151); Frank is venting his anger. The sheriff decides to 'let him get it out of his system' (p.153), the worst decision he has made so far. The reader suspects that Frank may do more than just smash glass but David's father comfortingly predicts that in the morning, 'Things will be back to normal' (p.154). He sends David back to bed, reassuring him that when he wakes 'the worst of this will all be over' (p.154). For this error of judgement they will all pay dearly. The nightmare has only just begun.

End of Part Three: Frank's suicide discovered (pp.154–162)

The two motifs of silence and light serve to heighten the drama of David's awakening on that fateful day. The silence from the basement probably woke David. The atmosphere is one of foreboding. There 'was no sunlight flooding my room' and the birds were silent in the face of the 'gray sky' (p.154). These repeated motifs of silence and light accentuate the seriousness of the consequences of Frank's suicide and heighten the suspense before Wesley goes to the basement.

David's reactions to the suicide

David thinks that today Frank will be jailed and realises that there will 'never be another day like it' (p.155) for his father. This is an accurate prophecy for when Wesley goes down to check on Frank, he cries out,

'Oh, no! *Oh my God, no!*' (p.159). David knows that this cry 'signalled such a breach in our lives, a chasm permanently dividing what we were from what we could never be again' (p.159).

David is jubilant. He can barely conceal his 'satisfaction over what had happened' because, in his naivety, he believes that 'Uncle Frank's suicide had solved all our problems' (p.161). While it is true that there will be no trial, no pressure on anyone to testify or be embarrassed or chastised (p.161), David is not experienced in the psychology of small town life. Very little can be hidden in a neighbourhood where the town's leaders are embroiled in sexual assault, murder and suicide, and Julian Hayden demonstrates his understanding of this later.

On the threshold of adulthood, David's belief that Frank's suicide will solve all their problems is the last thought of an innocent child. David, in maturity, will awaken to the harsh reality that loyalty to one's family can compromise justice, but also that the principle of moral absolutism is an ideal only.

Epilogue (pp.165–175)

The Epilogue summarises the aftermath of Frank Hayden's suicide which does not, as David had imagined, resolve all the problems besetting the family since Marie Little Soldier had fallen ill.

Who is to blame? (pp.165–168)

In his naivety, David thought that Frank's death would exonerate his father from all blame and that the townsfolk would never be asked to 'choose sides over guilt or innocence' (p.161). The latter proved correct, but not as David imagined. Julian Hayden deemed Wesley Hayden guilty. The verdict was that loyalty, especially to one's family, was more important than justice or doing the right thing. Julian could never understand how Wesley could choose the Indians in preference to his own brother. The opportunity for confronting racial prejudice was lost among the white townsfolk who closed ranks in support of Julian's power.

'It was decided' (p.165) that a tissue of lies about Frank's death would be concocted so that no blame fell on him or the family. The death would be classed 'accidental' and no mention of Frank's crimes would be made. But an unbridgeable gulf opened between Wesley and his father; the family was forced to move away from the townsfolk who supported Julian because of his power and domination.

In North Dakota, Wesley finally took the position of lawyer as Gail wished, but no one envisioned the price.

Young David's disbelief (pp.168–169)

As for the young David Hayden, he could not comprehend how:

> two people who only wanted to do right, whose only error lay in trying to be loyal to both family and justice, were now dispossessed … forced to leave Bentrock and build new lives. (p.169)

A part of him wanted momentarily to let his 'two hapless, forlorn' parents (p.169) leave Montana without him.

Remainder of the Epilogue (pp.169–175)

As for David Hayden after that, the dispossession of the family added to the accumulation of traumatic events, which dominated his formative years. His position as history teacher reflects his cynicism towards the recording of human history which omits ordinary people's 'stories of sexual abuse, murder, suicide' (p.170). He keeps a straight face and pretends that 'the text tells the truth, whole and unembellished' (p.170).

Something of the psychological damage inflicted on David can be gauged by the concealment of this story of abuse, power and corruption from his wife (p.174). The rather bleak summary, in contrast to the power of the Prologue, suggests how passive he is in regard to the past; he has repressed the pain and avoided dealing with his problems.

The deaths of Len, Julian and Wesley

The death of his father from cancer and the passing of both his grandfather and Len from strokes provided satisfactory metaphors for David. He attributes his father's cancer to the growing bitterness he carried within himself. He imagines the pressure of guarding their terrible secrets to be the reason for Julian and Len's cerebral hemorrhages (p.171).

Montana

David remembers his time with Marie Little Soldier with happiness because she had shown him that his life was not bound by 'blood or birthright' (p.173). It is ironic that David's freedom from the Hayden heritage, which might have been imposed on him, as it was on his father, is a result of the events of the summer of 1948. His father is adamant that Frank's death stems from the spiral of power and racial prejudice predominating in Bentrock rather than from living in the state of Montana: 'Don't blame Montana ... Don't ever blame Montana!' (p.175) were his indelible phrases, forever imprinted in the narrator's psyche.

Both David and Wesley Hayden love the land of their birthright, the open plains of northern Montana. It is not the *place* to which David can never return, but rather the people and the emotional scars they leave in the creation of their social history. In not blaming Montana, his father seems to seek some saving grace to ease the pain of the loss and humiliation he has suffered. While at one level the landscape cannot be 'blamed' for the human drama, which becomes human tragedy – such tragedies occur in other settings – this story does seem to suggest a parallel between the harshness of the landscape and the harshness of some of the inhabitants. Montana has demanded physical and mental toughness in those who wished to survive and dominate the land. For individuals like Julian Hayden, that toughness and need to dominate have taken over their whole lives.

CHARACTERS & RELATIONSHIPS

David Hayden

Social influences

The narrator is a twelve-year-old boy born before World War II, but growing up in its aftermath. David is part of a small family consisting of his paternal grandparents, his uncle and aunt and his parents. His maternal grand-mother of Norwegian ethnicity (p.64) and a maternal aunt who gave him a pair of moccasins (p.34) do not feature in the story. He has no siblings, no cousins with whom he can interact and no close school friends are apparent. Being an only child adds to a natural preference for isolation and his own company. His mother's fear of his being 'wild' (pp.21–22) is largely attributable to these circumstances. As he is more used to adult than to children's company, he is profoundly affected by adult behaviour.

From a perspective of maturity, the adult David is able to inform his readers about the intricate workings of a small town in the post-war American Wild West. This component of history makes the story intriguing, for the events of the summer of 1948 are locked into that particular geographical place and that specific era. David represents the third generation of the Hayden family in the town dominated by his grandfather. Julian Hayden followed the original settlers who wrested the land from the Indians; his father, Wesley, born in 1910 is also a product of his time and the characters' decisions reflect the nature of their history.

- See **Analysis** (p.9, Part One) for social influences on David.
- See novel (pp.21–24) for David growing up 'wild'.

Access to adulthood via eavesdropping

David is a pre-pubescent boy quickly approaching adolescence. He is a shy, serious boy and, without assistance from the adults in his life learns about adulthood by eavesdropping on adult conversations. By so doing he learns more than is appropriate for him to know.

As the story revolves around his perspective, the reader is limited by what David sees and, more particularly, by what he hears.

Loss of innocence

The central focus is David's encounter with adult corruption. As a twelve-year-old with time on his hands during the freedom of school holidays and with a yearning to be included in adult affairs – even to be accepted as an adult – David begins to eavesdrop when Marie Little Soldier becomes seriously ill. He learns of his Uncle Frank's sexual abuse and later it is he who reveals that Frank murdered his beloved Marie. He witnesses how his grandfather controls and influences the course of justice and how his own father's efforts to have justice brought to bear on his brother, Frank, falter because of divided loyalties between family and his responsibility to uphold the laws of the land as sheriff.

What David learns is shocking and the impact of 'guilty knowledge' on a twelve-year-old who has no one to interpret events for him is disturbing. Trace David's loss of innocence – and what this means for him – by looking at the following experiences and adding your own examples.

1 David's decision to stay and listen to his mother's account of Frank's sexual abuse of Indian women.

> I flinched and a part of me said leave, get away, run, now before it's too late, before you hear something you can't unhear. Before everything changes. But I pressed myself closer to the house and hung on. (p.47)

Consider how this knowledge changes his childhood world: he can no longer admire his charming and affable Uncle Frank, he is shocked at his mother's explicit sexual references, he realises his uncle is a pervert – his father's own brother – and has to reassess his father.

Because he cannot 'unhear' those first words describing Frank's sexual abuse of Indian women, he becomes caught in a web of knowledge that no longer allows him to ignore implications. Consequently, David cannot reclaim his childhood innocence – a very difficult life-lesson.

2 His desire to hear his father say that his Uncle Frank is innocent (p.54).

His father's silence condemns Frank. Note that the reader is left to infer the young boy's response from his breathless apprehension as he waits to hear his father say, 'of course I don't believe it; of course it isn't true' (p.54).

3 The shooting of the magpie (pp.81–82).

Here, he recognises that his pent-up feelings – sexual and emotional – are released through shooting; that he '*needed* [my emphasis] to kill something' (p.81). The accumulated and unexpressed emotions about 'Marie's illness, Uncle Frank's sins, and the tension between [his parents]' (pp.81–82) culminate in a strange state that violence releases. He realises 'unthought-of connections – sex and death, lust and violence, desire and degradation' (p.82) lie latent in every person, even the good and the 'innocent'. It is not the dead magpie that is significant for him as his half-hearted burying of it indicates; it is what the act of shooting has unleashed into his consciousness. He now realises how within even an apparently good heart there lies the potential to kill and that violence, sex, lust, desire and degradation are mysteriously linked in the human psyche.

4 His desire to shoot Frank (p.84).

His aiming of his rifle at Uncle Frank shortly after he shoots the magpie is done without even thinking of the consequences. Why? Is it that, subconsciously, another shooting might release his own confused feelings about Uncle Frank? Does this indicate that he wants to eliminate the problem by eliminating the person, rather than deal with issues? His learnt responses – that there will be serious consequences if you kill a human – are over-ridden by desires he didn't know he could have.

Again he learns about the shadow side, the unrecognised dark side of the human condition, something as a child he did not know.

5 His reaction to Julian's abuse of Wesley when Frank is imprisoned in the basement.

He wrongly fears that his grandfather is about to pull a gun on his father (p.116), then later overhears Julian firing verbal shots at Wesley. David then has to contend with this subtler and psychologically damaging form of violence. Does his response indicate both a loss of childhood innocence and a growing maturity?

6 His weeping because everything has changed – or appears to have changed for him and his family (p.125).

The escalating intensity of the problems with Frank in the basement and David being warned to keep Julian locked out of the house if he should come, leads to a further erosion of childhood innocence which he feels deeply. He doesn't weep for Marie who has died, or for Uncle Frank, or for anyone in the family. He weeps because 'the distance between us [his horse and himself] seemed too great for either Nutty and me to travel ever again' (p.125). He displaces all of his confused and unresolved feelings into this fear. Why? Possibly because his relationship with Nutty is one of unconditional love and that is what he needs now in the complicated adult world he has stumbled into. Perhaps, too, he now sees that his childhood desire to live with his horse is no longer even a possible thought. He has moved beyond the place of childish dreams – where pure and simple desires exist – into a sordid adult world of complicated needs, responsibilities and moral issues.

7 His sexual shame.

His first sexual stirrings in response to Aunt Gloria's naked breasts can be seen as innocent and natural, but after he learns of Frank's abuse of other girls and women he is too ashamed to even look at Aunt Gloria (p.78). Why do you think this is? Later, David finds himself looking anew at Miss Shott (p.128) and Lisa Waterman (p.129). Note his different responses and how his knowledge that Frank has molested women affects his own sexuality.

8 His belief that Uncle Frank's suicide will solve all family problems.

This probably reveals that knowledge can lead to loss of innocence but that knowledge does not ensure the development of maturity. David's growing maturity is uneven. For example, he can understand that one's birthright (being a Hayden, or an Indian) is beyond an individual's control. However, he is still too inexperienced of small town politics to comprehend that Uncle Frank's death will not reunite the family (p.167). Nor can he fully appreciate until he is adult that someone powerful and corrupt like Julian Hayden simply will not have his name, or favourite son's reputation, tarnished by a truth that in his eyes does not even constitute a crime.

David's sexuality

Uncle Frank's wife Gloria is the person David is first attracted to sexually in any conscious way. She is a tiny blonde woman, the opposite of Marie who is a six-foot earth mother, the first woman he sees naked. The adult David recognises that Marie was sexy but claims that as a twelve-year-old his love for her was chaste. What do you think? Does Marie's sexuality play any role in his life?

His Aunt Gloria is kind to David and he thinks she is beautiful. His sexuality is aroused when he sees her naked breasts one night when she is caring for him during a bout of tonsillitis. He is profoundly affected by this incident and later deeply saddened by Frank's sexual betrayal of Gloria. His secret knowledge of Frank's sexual abuse of women also seriously affects his own responses to women – his sexual responses are robbed of pleasurable innocence and encumbered with guilt and shame.

- See **Analysis** (p.13, Part One) David sees Marie Little Soldier naked
- See **Analysis** (p.24, Part Two) David's sexual feelings for Gloria
- See **Analysis** (p.25, Part Two) David concludes that sex, violence and death are closely aligned
- See **Analysis** (pp.34–35, Part Three) David's shame over his own sexuality

Gail Hayden's influence – David's relationship with his mother

The most influential person in David's life is his mother: an intelligent, non-prejudiced, upright moral citizen who is also a working mother. She is primarily responsible for his upbringing and conducts a loving, understanding relationship with her son.

David's mother was not raised in the harsh environment of Mercer County under the dominance of Julian Hayden. She is a strict Lutheran from a farm in a fertile valley in North Dakota and believes that they would all be happier if her husband was not the sheriff and did not live in Montana (p.19). She also thought it would have been better to raise her son in a larger community (p.24) to provide some curb on David's activities in the 'wild' country around Bentrock.

His welfare – physical, moral and spiritual – is her first concern and David's affection for Marie (as well as her own) motivate her to take up the cause of her brother-in-law's sexual abuse of Indian girls on the reservation. Indeed, it is because Marie is seen as physically commanding and, therefore, assumed to be able to take care of herself, that her revelations about Frank to Gail are the more astounding.

David's closeness to Gail is revealed in various ways. He is able to recognise her change of attitude towards Wesley as she fully realises what Frank's sexual crimes mean – Wes is not only her husband but 'a brother to a *pervert!*' (p.52) because they share the same feelings. He realises that she approaches problems such as the question of Frank's guilt in an intuitive way, for she is willing 'to go on ... her feelings, her faith' (p.53). She also openly shows her feelings towards her son with kisses and hugs, something his father does not do.

It is also his mother he approaches when he actively seeks to be included in adult affairs, but when he tries to raise the 'Frank issue' with her, she becomes evasive and disappoints him. As a young boy desperate to leave childhood behind, he fails to realise that she is trying to protect him from ignoble adult matters.

David, in his growing awareness of relationships between men and women, becomes aware of an attraction between his own mother and Len McAuley, believing that Len is probably in love with her (pp.94–95). He also thinks he is expected to form a new family with his mother and Len at one point. Consider how appropriate his responses are and see **Analysis** (pp.29–30, Part Two) for commentary on Len's feelings towards Gail Hayden.

Overall, David's relationship with his mother appears to be much stronger than that with his father.

David's relationship with his father – Wesley Hayden

David is disappointed in his father who does not fit the image of a sheriff of the Wild West and who fails to measure up against the charming war hero doctor, Uncle Frank. He wishes his father were more like Frank, even was Frank – yet he is also sympathetic to the role Julian has cast him in – the unrecognised, almost rejected son. As the story unfolds, David's understanding of his father increases. You can see some of these changes in the following selected examples:

- David notices his father's bad leg (p.38) and later links his father's sore knee with his father's anguish (p.100)
- he wants his father to be completely different from Frank (p.53); he sees similarity between Frank and Wes (p.84)
- his father's silence about Frank's guilt (p.54) – David's feelings?
- recognition that for Wesley, Julian is God (p.83)
- recognition of the difficulties and pain of being sheriff (p.90)
- jealousy in his father's voice (p.100)
- responses to his father's untypical behaviour – Wes's drunkenness (p.75); has Wes killed Frank? (p.109); talk about painting houses (p.113)
- his need for some physical show of affection from his father (p.154)
- attitude to Julian's treatment of Wes – at the park picnic (p.37); after Frank is put in the basement (pp.118–122; 123–124)
- attitude to his parent's hurt after the funeral (p.167)

- his refusal to become a lawyer or sheriff (p.170)
- his father shouting 'Don't blame Montana' (p.175).

It is his father's decisions, or lack of decisions, not his mother's, that are at the heart of the drama. Ironically though, his mother's naive, if moral, decision that justice can be done towards the favourite son of Julian Hayden proves to be the catalyst for Frank's 'arrest' and the catastrophe that follows. At twelve, David cannot participate in these decisions; he can only suffer the consequences with one important exception – telling his father he has seen Frank in their house the afternoon of Marie's death (p.96) and that Len, too, saw him (p.99). There is no doubt, however, that Wesley loves his son. As David realises, he is simply unable to demonstrate it (p.154). For David's view of his father see **Analysis** (p.10, Part One).

- In the Prologue David says he loves his father. Is that true?
- Does he respect his father?
- See **Analysis** (p.30, Part Two) for David's confession and manipulation of events.

Q Do you think David's disappointment about his father diminishes as he understands him better?

David and racial prejudice

David is also profoundly affected by the climate of racial prejudice towards the Indians. His grandfather's racism is a result of his being a settler who tamed the land and 'won' the plains of Montana from the Indians. Although a beneficiary of this action rather than a participant, as the sheriff of Mercer County his grandfather's views were formed by his place in history. David's own father is the son of this man and has inherited the view that Indians are useless and can only be productive citizens if they emulate the achievements of whites. David's own personal experience of Indians with Marie Little Soldier and Ronnie Tall Bear provide him with love, affection and a true sense of family and happiness. At the same time, he is aware that his uncle's sexual abuse of Indian women fits the wider definition of a human rights abuse.

- See **Racial Prejudice** (p.55) for a fuller discussion.

The adult David

We learn that David Hayden marries, becomes a history teacher, and rejects his father's professions of sheriff and lawyer. He seems to regard his youthful self with considerable sympathy and ironic detachment. He comments on the relationship between history and the truth – 'any human community might omit stories of sexual abuse, murder, suicide' (p.170). He puts the events of his own life into a context of concealment that perpetuates the myths that ordinary life is untroubled by such traumas. He has no desire to return to Bentrock in order to explore his past which suggests that, like his father, he probably avoids facing problems.

Wesley Hayden

David notes that his 'father was, in many respects, an impressive man. He was tall, broad-shouldered, and pleasant-looking'. This impression, however, does not dominate his recollections of his father who 'seemed somewhat prosaic ... stolid, surely, and steady and dependable. But inevitably, inescapably dull' (p.36). Furthermore, his father is not only physically crippled; he is a mental cripple, also, because of his upbringing. Not raised under the influence of any religion, he does not follow the kind of moral absolutism his wife does and it is his journey from ignorance to experience that underpins the central drama of the novel. This journey parallels David's from ignorance to knowledge. David also knows, from experience, that 'often he did not keep the promises' (p.67) he made.

- Trace the instances of how often these promises are not kept.
- Note he does not fit his wife's ideal either (p.19).

Wesley is the weaker son but he has the stronger moral sense. After Frank reveals the extent of his crime against Marie, Wesley and Gail's roles as the moral absolutes are reversed (p.150). Wesley's determination to bring his brother to justice becomes emphatic while Gail is ready to compromise and let Frank go.

Julian Hayden

Julian Hayden's influence in the town is evident long before he is introduced to the reader early in Part Two. He is a man governed by his need for power and this leads, inevitably, to corruption. (See **Themes & Issues**, 'Power and corruption', p.57, for an analysis of Julian Hayden.)

Both David's father and his uncle are products of an upbringing by a dominating father and a weak mother. As the long-serving sheriff of Mercer County and large landholder, Julian has left an indelible mark on all who come into contact with him. David knows that his influence is immense and that he is even more powerful than the law when he so chooses (p.129). The way Julian speaks to David's father leaves a lasting impression on David (p.116) who begins to understand the complexities of human relationships by seeing his grandfather interacting with his two sons. David's opinion about the relative strength and weakness of these two men constantly changes in the light of how much they are like, or unlike, Julian Hayden. Instead of always seeing them as opposites, David comes to appreciate their kinship as brothers. (For the contrast between the brothers see **Analysis**, p.15; for their likeness see **Analysis**, p.26.)

Although David loves visiting his grandfather's ranch for the freedom it gives him, he does not have a close relationship with him: his overbearing personality dwarfs the child's.

The dispossession of the family at the end of the story is solely the result of Julian Hayden's refusal to accept that Frank was guilty of rape and murder. Instead, he blames Wesley for Frank's death and, with his corrupt nature and entrenched racial prejudice, fails to understand why Wesley would support the cause of Indian girls.

Julian is an abhorrent character in the novel, a man with unbridled power who actively seeks dominance over his fellow humans and, in doing so, damages them irreparably.

Len McAuley

The Deputy Sheriff is a minor character but takes a crucial role in the story. He has bridged the reign of the father and son as sheriff and feels partly responsible for the final outcome. He feels he should have issued a warning about the upbringing of the brothers to Julian but has not dared. (See **Analysis**, pp.28–29, for Len's major role.) Len, together with his garrulous wife Daisy, holds the affections of David in place of loving grandparents (p.50). Len is a reformed alcoholic; it is implied that he became a drunk because he had to overlook Julian's corrupt behaviour as county sheriff.

Enid Hayden

David's grandmother plays only a minor role in both David's life and in his story. She is a quiet woman, her own personality subsumed under that of her overbearing husband. David describes her as 'a thin, nervous woman who seldom spoke when my grandfather was present' (p.76). He finds her 'pathetic' (p.76) but understands her subordinate role in an era before women's rights were recognised. Later David describes her as 'superstitious' (p.95) and has been encouraged to ignore her stories. After the family leaves Bentrock it is Enid, however, who continues to write to her son and visit them several times creating a link for David between the past and the present.

Gloria Hayden

David's aunt rarely appears with any substance in the story. She is a figure who is talked about by Julian and Wesley, and is the object of David's sexual fantasies and a model of sexual womanhood. Frank's and Gloria's wedding is recounted in retrospect to illustrate a case of racial prejudice by David's grandfather (p.76) and her inability to produce a grandchild is also discussed by Julian (p.71). Her barrenness is more symbolic of Frank's character than her own.

Note: all the Hayden women are represented as beautiful, contributing in a subtle way to the family's leadership image.

Frank Hayden

Although Frank is portrayed in glowing terms as a war hero, town doctor, sportsman and leading member of the community, the narrator constantly undercuts his character attributes. He remains an unsubstantial, rather shadowy figure, held at arm's length from the reader. His status in his father's eyes, in detriment to his brother, does not endear him to the reader. He has wit and charm, but the kind of charm which is shallow and insincere. (See also **Analysis**, pp.17–18, for further commentary on Frank.) Consider also the following:

- Gail is reserved towards him (p.44). She goes to Dr. Snow for medical treatment.
- David does not relate to him very well, despite being his only nephew (p.42) and Frank an attentive uncle (p.144).
- David does not trust him and does not want to be alone with him (p.41) when he has previously been comfortable with him. Why does he say this when he does not know yet that he has sexually abused Indian girls?
- Frank shows false concern for the Indians (p.42).

There are some unsatisfactory elements in regard to Frank, which the reader never fully understands:

- Why did he murder Marie when he knew that either a) Wesley would not pursue the charge of sexual abuse or b) his father would use his influence to defeat the charge?
- Why did he confess to Wesley that he had murdered Marie (p.149)?
- Why did he commit suicide when he thought his imprisonment was a joke?

Marie Little Soldier

Although she does not feature much in the story, Marie is the catalyst for the drama that revolves around her. It is her unease at Frank's attendance on her as a doctor which prompts the action, resulting in her confession of Frank's sexual crimes to Gail and then to Wesley. (See **Analysis**, pp.12–13, for her role in David's life.)

It is Marie's death that deepens the plot and leads to a charge of murder against Frank. This action, presaged in the Prologue, leads to David's philosophical exploration of what is the truth and what is a lie.

Ollie Young Bear

- See under **Themes & Issues** 'Racial Prejudice' (p.55).

Ronnie Tall Bear

- See under **Analysis** (p.13) and under **Themes & Issues** 'Sexuality/ Masculinity' (p.58).

THEMES & ISSUES

Racial prejudice

A significant undercurrent to the events of the summer of 1948 is racial prejudice. The citizens of Bentrock have inherited the nineteenth century view of the North American Indians as a people who, in Wesley Hayden's words are: 'ignorant, lazy, superstitious, and irresponsible' (p.34).

Following the wars between the white settlers and the Indian nations of North America, the Indian people were dispossessed of their lands and herded onto reservations without employment and with no means of the subsistence previously gained from the land.

By 1948 Indians were a marginalised race, pushed into areas of land which were of little use to whites, such as the reservation outside Bentrock. Untrained in European lifestyles, the native populations became a source only for cheap manual labour, such as Marie's position as a housekeeper in the Hayden household. David's father is the product of an upbringing and a society that sought to blame the victim and he can seems incapable of understanding a people with such a different culture from his own.

David begins to think about racial prejudice because of his affection for Marie Little Soldier. He realised that in Bentrock they were 'Objects of the most patronising and debilitating prejudice' (p.101) but were non-threatening towards the whites.

He does not understand either his father's, or his community's, attitude but he does recognise their hypocrisy. Ollie Young Bear is an acceptable member of the Indian community only because he conforms to a white ideal of 'what Indians *could* be' (p.58). He is a war hero, wounded in action; a university graduate; a deacon of the Lutheran church; a company executive; a star pitcher in a state baseball team; does not smoke, drink alcohol or swear; married a white woman from a prosperous family; has a boy and a girl. Indeed, he seems far too good to be true which is exactly what David thinks. In reality David finds him intimidating and dislikes him because 'he seemed to find no humor in the world' (p.59). But his father sees him as a perfect example of a successful Indian (albeit on white terms): 'He's a testimony to what hard work will get you' (p.58). David observes, however, that the Indians did not respect him for they believed 'He won't be happy until he's white' (p.60). By living as a white, Ollie Young Bear is betraying the ideals and culture of his own race.

Julian Hayden epitomises the attitude of superiority of the white race over the Indians. All his references to Indians are derogatory. He is obviously amused by Frank Hayden's preference for 'red meat' (p.72) and thinks there is nothing untoward about his sexual perversion: 'He had that little squaw down on her hands and knees' (p.72). As far as he is concerned, Frank's predilection for Indian girls is normal. He assumes that Gloria's lack of children is her fault and not Frank's because he supposes that there are some children on the reservation that look like Frank (p.72).

That these attitudes are entrenched is obvious and central to the drama of the novel. Gail Hayden's persuasion of Wesley that Marie Little Soldier has been sexually assaulted by Frank is at the heart of the story. Wesley wrestles with his conscience over the moral dilemma: should he charge his brother with the rape of Indian girls? This builds to the climax where Frank kills Marie by unexplained means. It is implied that Marie's death is horrible. Should the reader assume that Frank rapes Marie before he kills her?

Wesley's reaction to Frank's lack of remorse and to what he has told him could suggest this. Gail almost gags 'on what my father told her. Or on what he wouldn't tell her and what her imagination filled in' (p.150).

Gail Hayden provides the only role model for David who does not appear to be racist towards Indians. The novel shows no white males in David's world of Wild West Montana who are without racial prejudice.

Power and corruption

The society of Bentrock is dominated by the power of Julian Hayden. Although he lives out of town on his large ranch, nothing happens in the town outside the influence of David's grandfather. Julian Hayden's 'dude' ranch is ostentatious in the extreme, although the child David loves it. It is constructed of logs in imitation of the simple dwellings of the settlers but is actually a two-story mansion. The interior is entirely masculine with leather fittings featuring guns and animal trophies.

For years Julian reigned unopposed as the sheriff of Mercer County with Len McAuley as his deputy, while also managing his extensive landholdings. Although the position of sheriff is limited to three consecutive terms, Julian has managed to evade the red tape, notionally handing over to his deputy every six years for a term and then resuming his position. On retirement he passed his position to his son, Wesley. Although this is an elected position, the community would not dare to oppose a Hayden as sheriff.

David speculates on why his grandfather ever sought the position of sheriff in the first place. The answer is a simple one. 'He wanted, he needed, power. He was a dominating man who drew sustenance and strength from controlling others' (p.20). It was a natural progression from mastering the land to wishing to 'regulate the behavior of men and women' (p.20). It is this need to control which leads to the tragedy enacted in Bentrock in 1948.

David is acutely aware of his inheritance of the Hayden name and his family's importance in Mercer County:

> I was a Hayden. I knew ... without having been told, that that meant something in Bentrock. Because my grandfather was wealthy and powerful, because my father – like his father before him – enforced the law, because my uncle treated the sick and injured ... people had an opinion about the Haydens. (p.126)

No one, however, believes the Hayden influence to be a philanthropic one. Perhaps 'Grandfather bought someone's foreclosed ranch cheap or let his cattle graze someone else's range' (p.126) but the Haydens were 'as close as Mercer County came to aristocracy' (p.126). This gave David 'a measure of respect that … [he] didn't have to earn' (p.126).

But this kind of power that the Haydens possess leads to the corrupt behaviour at the core of the story. While Wesley has grown up in the shadow of his father, his wife Gail has been a moderating influence: at her instigation Wesley acts to bring his corrupt brother to justice. For Frank, the hero, possesses the epitome of a nature which has flourished under the influence of his father and his culture of corrupt morals and ideals. Wesley is a victim of that power and corruption. If David had grown to manhood in Bentrock, would he, too, have become sheriff and inherited the corruption which power inevitably brings?

Sexuality/masculinity

David is at the threshold of adolescence and his awakening sexuality underpins much of the action in the novel. It becomes clear that David lacks appropriate male role models. Use the following points to develop your own ideas on this issue.

No one, least of all his mother, would have him imitate his grandfather's ruthless quest for power and the defects of character that that implies. Julian is a stereotypical Wild West rancher, corrupted by his unchallenged domination over Mercer County. He is racist, swears, farts and regards women as inferior.

Uncle Frank is a war hero but that is where the heroic image stops. He is the son of his father and has inherited all the worst aspects of his father's character. Although he is the town doctor, married to a beautiful woman, he abuses his professional position by taking advantage of women from a deprived minority group. He has no moral standards that David can emulate.

Wesley Hayden is a weak man. His crippled leg has limited his status, but signifies more the crippling of his mind by Julian. He has inherited his father's position of power in the town and, although he does not abuse that position, he is still a town leader. When he is called upon to act for justice against corruption, he is weak and afraid of the power of his dominating father. David, in his new maturity, understands how difficult it must have been to be the son of Julian Hayden, 'to have a father capable of speaking to you' (p.116) in such an overbearing way. David is disappointed in his father, however, not least of all because he does not fulfil his idea of a Wild West sheriff. He does not tote a gun or carry out any significant arrests. He is just a small town sheriff keeping the peace (p.17). Even when Julian sends his men to forcibly break Frank out of the cellar, Wesley cannot be found and it is David's mother who attempts to ward off the intruders with a gun. Wesley only arrives after his deputy has intervened. Do you think David is left with a lasting impression of his father as weak when the family is forced to leave town? Does he feel that his father has so mishandled Frank's arrest that he is responsible for their forced departure from Bentrock?

Ollie Young Bear is an Indian whom David is expected to admire for all his remarkable achievements but David dislikes him because he treats him as a child and constantly criticises him when they go bowling. (See **Racial Prejudice**, p.55.) It is only Marie Little Soldier's boyfriend, Ronnie Tall Bear, whom David respects and admires for his freedom and athleticism. It is Ronnie and Marie who make him feel accepted for himself and not because of his birthright (p.173).

Apart from Marie's boyfriend all the male influence on David is towards the 'macho' image epitomised by his grandfather. While riding out from his grandfather's ranch, he takes the opportunity to improve his marksmanship with the new handgun his grandfather has given him. At twelve, David is a practised shot, although not always accurate. While shooting he kills a magpie and his emotions become mixed, linking sexuality with death and violence, lust, desire and degradation. He 'needed to kill something' (p.81) to release his mind from his thoughts of Uncle Frank's sexual crimes and from his own lustful thoughts about Frank's beautiful wife, Gloria.

Len McAuley is a supporter of both Julian Hayden and Wesley Hayden and has bridged both their regimes as sheriff. He is largely under Julian's power and is an alcoholic, probably because he has had to bury any manly ideals in the face of Julian's dominant personality. David, however, feels more affection for him than for his own grandfather, and would probably have acknowledged his positive contribution to his development.

The female influences in David's life are much more positive than the male. He loves his mother, Marie Little Soldier and Gloria Hayden. There is never any expression of love or affection for the males in his life even though he is sympathetic towards his father's predicament and understands the reasons for his weakness. He does say in the Prologue, however, that he loves his father but he is in a male environment where men simply do not show their deeper or gentler emotions very much. He does see his father crying but it was his ageing that dominated David's response, not his emotional state.

Finally consider what is revealed of the adult David and what kind of male he has become. Whose influences seem most apparent?

Violence and sexual abuse

An underlying current of violence pervades the story from the Prologue on. There is the image of a delirious Marie Little Soldier and her fate is mentioned; the narrator's father is kneeling, 'frantic' (p.11); his mother loads a shotgun; the sound of breaking glass; and the odour of rotting vegetables. The story is based on a case of sexual abuse, which becomes murder. Suicide follows culminating in the narrator's family's dispossession.

The thread of sexual abuse and sexuality which run through the book are linked to the inferior position that all the women of Mercer County hold, but particularly that of the Indian women who inhabit the nearby reservation and the fringes of the town. Most of the white male characters, with the exception of the narrator, do not appear to hold women in high esteem. Perhaps Gail Hayden commanded more respect – she is a 'working woman' at a time when women were encouraged to stay at home and bear children.

Julian Hayden epitomises the male aggression towards the female inherent in this Wild West community. He even refers to his own daughter-in-law in terms of grave disrespect, doubting that her failure to reproduce is because she is of small build for she certainly has 'enough tit for twins' (p.71). He debases Indian women as 'squaws' and 'red meat' (p.72).

Both the narrator's father and uncle make fun of Marie's refusal to see a doctor, believing that she is merely 'superstitious' (p.35) with experience of only the tribe's medicine man rather than a qualified white medical practitioner. Marie's adamant pleas against Frank's visit are not seen as a woman's right to privacy and control over her own body; they are seen as 'ignorance'.

The Hayden males see the consequent revelations of rape and sexual assault against Indian girls as trivial. It is only through Gail Hayden's moral perspective that the sheriff is persuaded to view Frank Hayden's crimes with any seriousness. Ultimately, the novel reveals how sexual abuse remains a hidden crime, its revelation prevented by powerful white males like Julian Hayden.

Loyalty and justice

Much of the action revolves around loyalty to one's family versus justice for a minority group.

- Follow Wesley Hayden's dilemma of which master he should serve: family or the law.
- What is Gail Hayden's role in his decision?
- On which side does David/adult narrator stand?
- Would the town have reacted differently if the case of sexual assault had been against a white woman?

Finally, justice has not been served and family loyalty has been compromised. There appear to be no winners or losers when these two issues are opposed.

QUESTIONS & ANSWERS

This section focuses on your own analytical writing on the text, and gives you strategies for producing high-quality responses in your coursework and exam essays.

Essay writing – an overview

An essay on a literary work is a formal and serious piece of writing that presents your point of view on the text, usually in response to a given topic. Your 'point of view' in an essay is your interpretation of the meaning of the text's language, structure, characters, situations and events, supported by detailed analysis of textual evidence.

Analyse – don't summarise

In your essays it is important to avoid simply summarising what happens in a text.

- A **summary** is a description or paraphrase (retelling in different words) of the characters and events. For example: 'Macbeth has a horrifying vision of a dagger dripping with blood before he goes to murder King Duncan.'
- An **analysis** is an explanation of the real meaning or significance that lies 'beneath' the text's words (and images, for a film). For example: 'Macbeth's vision of a bloody dagger shows how deeply uneasy he is about the violent act he is contemplating – as well as his sense that supernatural forces are impelling him to act.'

A limited amount of summary is sometimes necessary to let your reader know which part of the text you wish to discuss. However, always keep this to a minimum and follow it immediately with your analysis of what this part of the text is really telling us.

Plan your essay

Carefully plan your essay so that you have a clear idea of what you are going to say. The plan ensures that your ideas flow logically, that your argument remains consistent and that you stay on the topic. An essay plan should be a list of **brief dot points** – no more than half a page.

Include your central argument or main contention – a concise statement (usually in a single sentence) of your overall response to the topic. Also write three or four dot points for each paragraph indicating the main idea and evidence/examples from the text. Note that in your essay you will need to *expand* on these points and *analyse* the evidence.

Structure your essay

An essay is a complete, self-contained piece of writing. It has a clear beginning (the introduction), middle (several body paragraphs) and end (the last paragraph or conclusion). It must also have a central argument that runs throughout, linking each paragraph to form a coherent whole.

The introduction establishes your overall response to the topic. It includes your main contention and outlines the main evidence you will refer to in the course of the essay. Write your introduction *after* you have done a plan and *before* you write the rest of the essay.

The body paragraphs argue your case – they present evidence from the text and explain how this evidence supports your argument. Each body paragraph needs:

- **a strong topic sentence** (usually the first sentence) that states the main point being made in the paragraph
- **evidence** from the text, including some brief quotations
- **analysis** of the textual evidence explaining its significance and **explanation** of how it supports your argument
- **links back to the topic** in one or more statements, usually towards the end of the paragraph.

Connect the body paragraphs so that your discussion flows smoothly. Use some linking words and phrases like 'similarly' and 'on the other hand', though don't start every paragraph like this. Another strategy is to use a significant word from the last sentence of one paragraph in the first sentence of the next.

Use key terms from the topic – or synonyms for them – throughout, so the relevance of your discussion to the topic is always clear.

The conclusion ties everything together and finishes the essay. It includes strong statements that emphasise your central argument and provide a clear response to the topic.

Avoid simply restating the points made earlier in the essay – this will end on a very flat note and imply that you have run out of ideas and vocabulary. The conclusion is meant to be a logical extension of what you have written, not just a repetition or summary. Writing an effective conclusion can be a challenge. Try using these tips:

- Start by linking back to the final sentence of the second-last paragraph – this helps your writing to 'flow', rather than leaping back to your main contention straight away.
- Use synonyms and expressions with equivalent meanings to vary your vocabulary. This allows you to reinforce your line of argument without being repetitive.
- When planning your essay, think of one or two broad statements or observations about the text's wider meaning. These should be related to the topic and your overall argument. Keep them for the conclusion, since they will give you something 'new' to say but still follow logically from your discussion. The introduction will be focused on the topic, but the conclusion can present a wider view of the text.

Essay topics

1 'David moves from innocence to knowledge but not to maturity.' Do you agree?

2 "I realized that these strange, unthought-of connections – sex and death, lust and violence, desire and degradation – are there, there, deep in even a good heart's chambers." In your view, of what significance is this realisation in David Hayden's life?

3 'Although David says in the prologue that he loved his father, ultimately he appears to be disappointed in him.' Do you agree?

4 How do racist attitudes to Indians contribute to the catastrophe that overtakes the Hayden family?

5 Julian Hayden "needed power ... [he] drew strength from controlling others". How does David's grandfather dominate the story of Montana in 1948?

6 'David Hayden lacks positive male role models.' Discuss.

7 Marie Little Soldier and Gloria Hayden are David's ideal women. Discuss their importance in David's life in Montana in 1948.

8 Why does Wesley Hayden wish his wife "had not told the sheriff" about his brother's sexual abuse of Indian girls?

9 Frank Hayden is charming and witty with a personality that "glittered". Why, then, does the reader find him a rather repellent character?

10 'Exposing the truth and doing the "right thing" are shown to be impossible in Bentrock in 1948.' Do you agree?

Analysing a sample topic

Julian Hayden "needed power ... [he] drew strength from controlling others". How does David's grandfather dominate the story of Montana in 1948?

For a comprehensive answer you should know your text thoroughly and understand all parts of the question. Use these notes to develop an essay. Refer to the text appropriately using short quotes.

- It is a good idea to define first, for yourself, the key words in the topic such as 'power', 'controlling' and 'dominate'.
- You need to show that you agree/disagree with the contention, but in this case it is obvious that David believes his grandfather is powerful and that he can even override the law if necessary. (Perhaps support with a quote from p.122: 'Stop this before I have to'.)
- You need to show how the author has developed the character. Importantly, Julian does not appear in person until Part Two so you could follow through the passages where he is mentioned in Part One. These demonstrate that he is a main player in events in David's mind.
- Julian Hayden's authority has been established in the town two generations before David. You could refer briefly to how his position as the sheriff of Bentrock was achieved, maintained and then passed on to his son. Comment on whether David thinks this involved corruption.
- Show how you think Julian Hayden has governed the upbringing of his sons and the consequences that arise from such a parental influence. You could comment here on his moral values and on his differing treatment of Wesley and Frank. Here you could quote Len McAuley's observations to David (see p.94).
- To further develop your argument you could give your impressions of how David both sees his grandfather and is influenced by him. You might refer to the passage where Julian gives David a hand gun to 'blast' coyotes but David already has an arsenal and realises this

is different; it is 'for shooting as an activity in itself' (p.80). You might want to refer here to the consequences of this gift.

- Finally, you need to show whether or not Julian's domination of events in Bentrock in 1948 changes the course of history for David and how this is achieved.
- Your conclusion could include a pertinent quote that reinforces the point that Julian Hayden 'needed power' and that such unbridled power leads to the corruption of moral values.

REFERENCES & READING

The text

Watson, Larry, *Montana 1948*, Pan Books, London, 1995.

Other references

Brown, Dee, *Bury My Heart at Wounded Knee*. Any edition.

Watson, Larry, *Justice*, Milkweed Editions, Minneapolis,1995. This is a prequel to *Montana 1948*.

Watson, Larry, *White Crosses*, Pocket Books, 1997. Also set in Mercer County, the main protagonist is a sheriff. Similar themes are explored here.

Film

The Searchers 1956, directed by John Ford, starring John Wayne. This film gives you a classic movie construction of the 'Wild West'. You could compare some of the ideas of the 'Wild West' in the novel with their representation in the film.

Websites

For details of the Wounded Knee Massacre, see

www.linecamp.com/museums/americanwest/western_places/wounded_knee_massacre/wounded_knee_massacre.html

For details of Custer's Last Stand: Battle of the Little Big Horn, see

www.linecamp.com/museums/americanwest/western_places/little_big_horn_custers_last_stand/little_big_horn_custers_last_stand.html